COL J. R. Snowden
Director of Evaluation
The Ordnance School
Aberdeen Proving Ground
Maryland
October 1981

The Big Shots

The Big Shots

Edwardian Shooting Parties

Jonathan Garnier Ruffer

Debrett–Viking Press

*This book is dedicated to
my father and Sir Humphrey Tollemache
to both of whom I owe so much.*

First published December 1977
Second printing March 1978
Third printing August 1978

© Copyright Jonathan Garnier Ruffer 1977

ISBN 0-670-16376-7

Printed in Great Britain

Library of Congress catalog card number: 78-69891

Contents

Acknowledgements *6*

Introduction by Lord Walsingham *7*

1 The Rise of the Shoot *11*

2 The Royal Example *19*

3 The Great Shots *41*

4 Famous Shoots *54*

5 The Foreigner as Host and Guest *70*

6 Proprieties and Improprieties *82*

7 The Supporting Cast *111*

Appendix 1. Records *133*

Appendix 2. Lord Ripon on How to Shoot *137*

Index *141*

Acknowledgements

My thanks go to Lord Albemarle, the Nuns at Alresford, Mrs. Ronnie Archdale, Annie Benson, Julian Browning, Barbara Cartland, Nicholas Chance, Noel Cunningham-Reid, Lord Coke, Robin d'Abo, Andrew Dalton, James Denker, the Duke of Devonshire, Jonathan Ellis, the Rev. Jonathan Fletcher, Major Garnier, the late John Gladstone of Capenoch, the Hon. Richard de Grey, Holland and Holland Ltd., Lady Ingilby, Robert Jarman, Patsy, Lady Jellicoe, William Keith Neal, the Duke of Marlborough, Charles Mason, Sir Mark Milbank, Mrs. Jack Millar, Mary, Duchess of Roxburghe, the *Shooting Times*, and Lord Swinton. Particular thanks to John Richards for his invaluable help with material on Sir Ralph Payne Gallwey, and to Anita Leslie for a great deal of help and encouragement. I should also like to thank Count Paul Raben for the use of his library, and both Geoffrey Jaques and David Grief, without whose tolerance and telephone I should have been lost. For pictures, I am grateful to *Country Life* (a very big thank you to Pennie Cunliffe Lister for her help), the Mansell Collection, Popperfotos, the Radio Times Hulton Picture Library, and Nicholas Chance.

I am grateful to the following for permission to quote from their books: Adam and Charles Black: *The Shotgun*, by T. D. S. and J. A. Purdey; Curtis Brown Ltd.: *Recollections of Three Reigns*, by Sir F. Ponsonby; Faber and Faber Ltd.: *Men, Women and Things*, by the Duke of Portland; The Earl of Fingall and Pamela Hinkson: *Seventy Years Young*, by Daisy, Countess of Fingall; Wm. Heinemann Ltd.: *The Glitter and the Gold*, by Mrs. Consuelo Balsan; Hutchinson and Co. Ltd.: *It Was Such Fun*, by Mrs. Hwfa Williams, *Arthur James Balfour*, by Mrs. E. C. Dugdale, *Edwardians in Love*, by Anita Leslie, *Mr. Frewen of England*, by Anita Leslie; John Murray Ltd.: *From My Private Diary*, by Daisy, Princess of Pless; Putnam & Co: *Edwardian Heydays*, by George Cornwallis-West.

And, lastly, my thanks to Yvonne and Jan, whose enthusiastic typing left only a little to be desired.

Introduction

Here is a collection of reminiscences of an age which now is history. It will serve as a reminder, for those who are minded to pursue the bye-ways of social history, of a period rich in character and eccentricity when the pace of living followed a more humane scale than today and leaders of thought and action had time for lengthy recreations. But I would be doing the author a disservice if I were to give the impression that his book was intended primarily as a contribution to social history. It is written with a lightness of touch (and an ever so slightly waspish interest in the gossip) which makes it ideal bedside reading, or at least the kind of book which can be browsed through rather than studied at length.

Some of the limelight is enjoyed by my great uncle Tom de Grey, 6th Lord Walsingham, who excelled in knocking birds out of the sky, as well as with bat and ball, and vied with the monarch and his namesake Earl de Grey for recognition as the best shot in the land. So far as my great uncle was concerned it was a matter to be taken very seriously, although without undue importance. He would put himself out to establish the record for grouse shot in one day by having every bird on his Yorkshire estate driven over him, with a plan of campaign more appropriate to a battle between nation-states and every tactical consideration given due weight. He would record in framed manuscript, with what he took to be suitable illuminations in his own hand – and with evident satisfaction, the 1,070 grouse shot to his own pair of guns in 14 hours 18 minutes. I quote: 'No shot fired but by me . . . once I killed 3 birds at one shot – the only 3 in sight at the time – and 3 times I killed 2 at one shot, each time intentionally.' They were hearties, accustomed to kicking and being kicked; one gets the impression you would not have scored by being backward in coming forward; you made your bid and pushed it for all it was worth, or a little more sometimes. They were also rib-nudgers and practical jokers; their humour tended to be personal even if generally without malicious intent.

In these more intellectually sophisticated times – of course I do not suggest we dress as well – it is tempting to dismiss much of the Edwardian amusements Mr. Ruffer has captured for us as high-class buffoonery. But there was another side to it. Like the old Lord Warwick on page 88, 'I have come to the conclusion, being no longer young and a staunch conservative' that the Norfolk worthies come out of it quite well, compared with some of the bounders in the shires. If so, I am confirmed in my prejudice that Norfolk is the most civilised (or the most uncivilised?) county in the country. Or is it that Mr. Ruffer, who is I suspect no foreigner to the county, has simply seen to it that the whig dogs do not have the best of it? Whichever way it be, it is necessary to remind ourselves that many of the characters round whom Mr. Ruffer has woven his story were men of distinction in their day, their warts notwithstanding. In my great uncle's case he rested his claim to fame on his scientific work as an ornithologist and lepidopterist to establish, following Alfred Russell Wallace his elder contemporary, the variety and gradual mutability of species first documented by Wallace with Charles Darwin. I possess the first edition of his study of Hawaiian Microlepidoptera (illustrated with 448 colour prints of their wings) in which he identifies 62 genera and 441 species of small moths at that time resident in the islands – a descriptive work of little merit in itself but immensely painstaking, and trail-breaking in its way. He analyses these moths into three groups of species, those of American origin most closely similar to American species, those from south East Asia, and an indigenous group, remnants he suggests of the species formerly inhabiting a Pacific land mass of which only the mountain tops have survived inundation. That such gentlefolk found time for this kind of cataloguing, and at the same time (in my great uncle's case) could write with Sir Ralph Payne Gallwey the two volumes of the Badminton Library on Shooting (Field and Covert) and Shooting (Moor and Marsh) indicates – amongst other things – a golden age for the amateur scientist. This amateurism, now a dirty word, was not of a dilettantist kind; it was merely typical of a time when science proceeded without undue dependence upon plant and stupendous budgets. The same freedom is now probably enjoyed by students of abstract mathematics and philosophies alone.

His Lordship's framed grouse record now hangs in the lavatory at Merton Hall – the decision of the hanging committee being more influenced by his later financial unsuccess than by any intrinsic flaw in its design. He gambled heavily on converting Walsingham House in Piccadilly into a club and hotel (now the Ritz Hotel) and his debts eventually led to the breaking of the entail on his estates and the relative impoverishment of his posterity. His marital infidelities also were remarkable, in an age when infidelity was commonplace; though the scandal was for the most part confined to the locality since it seems he usually slept with his housemaids. He left no legitimate issue.

8

Most of the company who appear in the pages of this book were of more public interest than my great uncle – and I am therefore privileged to be invited to write this introduction. For those sufficiently interested in the shooting which informed the parties, I can not do better than recommend for further reading the two Badminton Library volumes mentioned above, which although out of print can often be picked up from a good second-hand bookseller.

Merton Hall, Thetford, Norfolk   WALSINGHAM
August, 1977

The shooting party 1913: with
the Duke of Portland at
Welbeck.

1
The Rise of the Shoot

A change happened in England about the 1860s. Previously gentlemen had walked through woods and shot pheasants as they flew away. Now it was the estate workers who did the walking, driving the pheasants towards the gentlemen, who stood the other end. It was a simple rearrangement, but the principle of the driven bird had far-reaching social consequences. In 1820 Bishop Latimer had written, 'Hunting is a good exercise for men of rank, and shooting an amusement equally lawful and proper for inferior persons.' Three-quarters of a century later it was the way in which all the great landowners entertained throughout the winter months.

The railway helped; so did the technical improvement of the gun. The one made the shooting estates more accessible, the other extended the scale of the carnage and touched it with artistry. Statistics mattered in this competitive affair, and so did social style – you combined the opportunities of a Vimy Ridge machine-gunner with an infinitely better lunch. And to bless these questionable endeavours was the accolade of the Prince of Wales's passion for the sport. It was natural that society should exert itself in pursuits which its champion made fashionable. The Prince, later King Edward VII, had neither the shape nor the temperament for the hunting field. The organised shoot was ideal – its pleasures were admirably exclusive and wonderfully extravagant.

No expense was spared. The scale of the major shoots was staggering. It even caused some bankruptcies, Lord Walsingham and the Maharajah Duleep Singh among them, but in an age when income tax was 5d. in the pound, the resources of the very rich could withstand extraordinary demands. Armies of gamekeepers and estate workers were involved, and the number of birds reared increased dramatically. By 1900 Sandringham alone was rearing 12,000 pheasants a year – and this in addition to the wild birds on the estate and the partridges and hares already to be found there. The theories developed by individual estates survive today in the lessons of, for

11

The early days: a sport for all sorts and conditions of men.

instance, the Euston or the Elveden System. They are a far cry from the first beginnings of the organised shoot, a haphazard attempt to rear some pheasants for a few days' sport, with the assistance of a handyman to look after the birds and keep down the vermin. In some cases the stock would be further augmented on the day of the shoot by quantities of fully grown pheasants, delivered by train and released in the coverts before the guests arrived. You could not admit to the practice, but no one could tell the difference – except on one recorded occasion when the railway authorities rather insensitively clipped the pheasants' wings to help with the train journey.

It is the gun's development that we should perhaps consider first, since the capacity of small numbers of people to kill large numbers of birds was the essence of what smart Edwardians understood to be a successful shoot. On the sophistication of the gun itself depended the technique of those who used it. The other ingredients of the shoot were simply a matter of money, organisation and social position.

The developments themselves began in the thirteenth century, when an English monk, Roger Bacon, invented gunpowder – though it was a long time before it was put to sporting use. For generations the gentleman's preoccupation with pheasants and partridges was for hawking rather than shooting, and it was not until the end of the eighteenth century that the firing-piece became sufficiently reliable to attract the leisured classes into the ranks of the sporting shots. By 1792 George Montagu could write in the *Sportsman's Directory*: 'The rage for shooting was never at a higher pitch than at present . . . the art of shooting flying is arrived at tolerable perfection.' By present day standards the claim seems ambitious. The flintlock gun of this period must have been a difficult weapon even to fire.

A sportsman had first to remove the powder from a flask, secondly to ram a thick wad down the barrel, thirdly to measure the shot from

The pheasantries at Sandringham.

Advertisement for 1910.

13

a pouch, fourthly to ram another thin wad down, and fifthly to put the caps on the nipples. To save time, a good loader carried the wads in his mouth. Not surprisingly, the sportsman was at the mercy of the elements. His principal enemy was rain. Damp in the lock of the gun would guarantee a misfire, and was no help to the gunpowder. One man at Windsor in the 1830s, refusing to be deterred by wet weather, trudged fruitlessly over the estate after partridges and eventually conceded defeat when he leant over the muzzle of his gun to reload and a torrent of water tipped from the rim of his bowler hat straight down the barrel.

There were other hazards, too. It was unwise, for instance, to hold the left hand too far down the barrel, since the gun was liable to burst. But the most difficult feature of all was the period of time which elapsed between the pulling of the trigger and the charge leaving the muzzle of the gun. The 'hang fire' of the flintlock caused by this slow ignition of the powder meant that any bird not flying directly away from the marksman was a particularly difficult shot. It was a problem only resolved with the advent of the percussion gun, which was slow to appear considering that the principles on which the percussion cap was based had been known for a very long while. Indeed in Pepys's *Diary* there is the following entry: 'At noon, to coffee house, where with Dr. Allen, some good discourse about physic and chemistry. And among other things I telling him what Dr. Dribble, the German doctor, do offer of an instrument to sink ships, he tells me that which is more strange, that something made of gold, which they call in chymestry *aurum fulminans*, a grain, I think, he said it was, put into a silver spoon and fired will give a blow like a musquett and strike a hole through the silver spoon downwards without the least force upwards.'

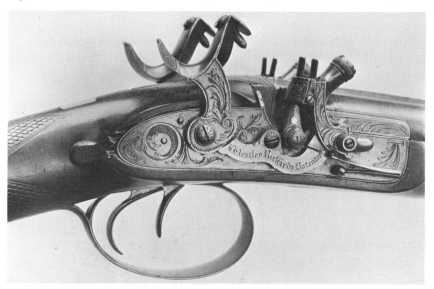

A hammer gun by Westley Richards.

The percussion gun was still loaded from the muzzle and it was not until the 1850s that the first breechloaders began to be seen on the shooting field. The duellists, for whom the hang fire effect involved more serious consequences, caught on to the new development more urgently than the sportsmen, and in the rural areas the breechloader at first caused consternation. (One keeper was heard to exclaim, 'Lor! He's 'bin and broken his gun the very first shot!') But the innovation, once accepted, enabled driven shooting to develop more quickly than ever before and this in turn generated still further improvements in the gun. From the 1870s onwards hammerless guns became popular; later still came the ejector, and the single-trigger gun. By the turn of the century the shotgun, to borrow a phrase from George Montagu, had 'arrived at a tolerable perfection'. In essentials it has not been improved since.

While those new to the sport would prefer the most up-to-date equipment, there are interesting examples of how the established shots tended to be more conservative. Lord Ripon continued to shoot with hammer guns until his death in 1923, and Lord Walsingham said he could shoot better with them than with anything else. King George v continued with hammer guns probably later than anyone, still shooting with them at the end of his life in 1936. It seems that the presence of hammers on the outside of the gun enabled him to get a quicker alignment on the birds. These hammer guns were specially built for him by Purdey, who also provided them with ejectors.

Lord Ripon (as Lord de Grey) provides another example of this same conservatism. In the 1880s Colonel Schultz introduced a new smokeless powder. It was an enormous improvement, since the old-fashioned black powder, apart from being unreliable, obscured the vision of the shooter after he had fired one shot. (It could be even more dramatic: Lord Walsingham set fire to himself and his loader in a butt when his powder burst into flames, and they were lucky to escape with only singed eyebrows.) Although Lord Ripon was to describe the Schultz powder as being superior in its 'practical absence of smoke, its gentle recoil, and its silent discharge', it was some years before he tried it. He wrote to Mr Athol Purdey, the gunmaker, in 1894: 'I was much pleased with the Schultz powder you sent me. I find I shoot at least 30% quicker with it than the black. I am not quite so accurate as yet, but I made up the more by the number of shots got off. My bag may interest you: 12th August, de Grey – 34, 71, 87, 92, 53, 74, 54, 57, 80, 43, equals 650 grouse; 14th August de Grey – 30, 40, 48, 111, 90, 70, 80, 31, equals 500. Total, 2 days, 1,150. Please send me 2,000 of the same cartridges to be here by the 24th August.' This letter has an additional interest in that it shows the new powder must have called for a different style of shooting, since the writer says it is taking him some time 'to get the hang of it'.

Possibly the last photograph of King George v as Prince of Wales, May 1910. The hammers on his Purdey are clearly shown.

15

The growth of the Railway: the opening of the Glasgow and Gainkirk Railway, 1831.

Though nobody would have been shooting seriously with muzzle loaders by the end of the century, they enjoyed a final moment of royal patronage according to an entry in the Sandringham game book for 6 December 1907: 'Prince Edward [King Edward VIII] and Albert [King George VI] fired their first shots out of a small single muzzle loader being the same gun which His Majesty King Edward, the late Duke of Clarence and the Prince of Wales [King George V] fired their first shots.' It is a dutiful note on which to leave the development of the gun for another factor in the shooting party phenomenon – the railway.

By the 1870s, the railway companies had appreciated that there was a need to build luxurious trains for the transportation of the aristocracy. They had to contend with some formidable prejudices: the 5th Duke of Portland, for example, was unwilling to be seen by the railway staff, and so had a railway carriage built to accommodate his own barouche. The carriage caught fire in a tunnel and His Grace had to be removed bodily by those very underlings he was so determined to avoid. Another train, which left Euston Station on 1 August 1873, was more typically smart, though no more fortunate. It carried Sir John Anson and Lady Florence Leveson-Gower, who were on their way to a shooting houseparty in the north with the Duke of Suther-

16

land. The sixteen carriages were all luxuriously built, even those reserved for the staff, with special quarters for the dogs and ample accommodation for the baggage. The train was capable of 50 m.p.h., the speed at which it was travelling when, passing through Wigan station, it was accidentally derailed. There were fatalities among the staff; the shooting party 'regulars' escaped. (Indeed, only Lord Bertie Vane-Tempest within that category was to die in a railway accident, and that was not until 1921.)

When Sandringham was bought by the Prince of Wales in the 1860s, he had a railway station built at Wolferton to bring his guests as conveniently near the house as possible. It showed that the railway, that dubious innovation which had been introduced between Stockton and Darlington a generation before, was now respectable. Aristocratic disapproval, which had been a real problem at the beginning, had evaporated when it became clear how much money was to be made from parting with land for the railways. As the network developed, it became possible to travel to houses which were further away, and each guest could be assured that no crisis could arise in London to which he could not return in a matter of hours. For the first time many important public figures were enticed away from London for a weekend. They came; they enjoyed themselves. The hosts grew bolder; the next invitations were for a week and still they were accepted. Sometimes, of course, it was necessary for one of the guests to rush back on business, but a sudden departure needed a

Arrival: a typical country station, *circa* 1900.

valid excuse – and certainly better than this one provided by Mr. Washington Hibbert when staying in Norfolk. The morning after his arrival he announced that he was leaving at once, saying to his host, 'My dear fellow, I am leaving because the entrée was so cold at dinner it made my teeth ache all night.'

One of the reasons that shoots in the north of Scotland took so long to develop was that the railways were slow to penetrate to that part of the world. The south of Scotland was comparatively accessible, even from London. It was possible to shoot a left and right of grouse on a Perthshire moor only sixteen hours after leaving Euston Station, and consequently the most sophisticated Scottish sportsmen were to be found there. On the west, for many years the furthest north that the railways ventured was Fleetwood in Lancashire, because of the problem of passing Shap Fell. Any sportsman who wished to travel to the west or north of Scotland was forced to get out at Fleetwood, and board a slow steamer which crawled up the west coast of Scotland in very much the same way as small craft had done for centuries.

Crucial though they were to the development of the great shoots, the improved techniques of the gunsmith and the availability of the railways were only a part of the story. They made the occasion possible, they did not in themselves make it desirable. For this a social impetus was needed, and this was provided principally by the Prince of Wales and his immediate circle.

Euston Station 1900.

2
The Royal Example

Queen Victoria was not a figure around whom society could easily form. By nature humourless, her severity increased following the death of her husband, the Prince Consort. She rarely came to London after this, preferring to attend to her duties from Windsor, or from the rambling and unattractive house at Osborne on the Isle of Wight, where she was eventually to die. The consequence was that she lost touch with her subjects. A command to dine at Windsor was increasingly seen as a necessary evil rather than a pleasure and an honour. Some of the Queen's guests could scarcely contain their boredom. Daisy Brooke, commanded to attend a banquet on the night before the Essex Hunt Races, one of the highlights of the sporting year, left Windsor Castle at dawn the following day, dressed in hunting pink. Her boldness did not pass unnoticed: Queen Victoria, watching in her nightgown from behind a curtain, was very shocked, and remarked to her lady-in-waiting, 'How fast, how very fast.'

But nobody wanted to be slow. As the Prince of Wales grew to manhood, society looked to him for a lead. That his life style was going to be very different was apparent from an early age. A friendship with a certain actress named Nellie Clarke in 1861 was much talked about, and even if his mother described it as being caused by 'wicked wretches who had led our poor boy into a scrape which caused his beloved father and myself the deepest pain' (though both of them had forgiven him 'the one sad mistake'), it quickly became obvious that this was no isolated incident. The season of 1864, the year of the wedding of the Prince and Princess of Wales, was unusually lively, as if its participants sensed a fundamental change in outlook. From that date, the ascendancy of the Prince of Wales over society was complete until his death nearly fifty years later. His personal tastes, and in particular his love of shooting, became the tastes of his smarter and richer subjects.

The Queen's refusal to include him in even the most mundane of public affairs, and the fact that, as a member of the Royal Family, he

Society leaders: the Prince and Princess of Wales in 1870.

Edward as a sportsman: his love of shooting started at an early age.

High jinks in Scotland. The Prince enjoys himself.

could not take an active part in political life, had meant that he had to develop other interests. His father had early introduced him to the pleasures of the chase, taking him stalking on the recently acquired Balmoral estate. At any rate, by the time the Prince went on the Near East tour which was hastily arranged for him following his father's death, it was clear that his passion for shooting was well developed. The reports of that trip show that he exercised his skill in a fairly haphazard way: wild boars, owls, crocodiles, quail – anything that moved received a royal salute. It began to show at home as well. It was no coincidence that the property which Edward obtained at Sandringham was in the best shooting country in England, and he was at the forefront of the development of driven shooting. The words which Lord Warwick wrote at the beginning of his autobiography could easily have been written by King Edward: 'I have carried out my official duties as long and as faithfully as I can, and for the rest I have lived in such fashion as seemed most agreeable to me . . . convinced that a good day's shooting is second in point of pleasure to nothing else on earth.' What Edward pioneered at Sandringham, was followed on numerous other estates. We can follow the King on his tour of them – Merton, Holkham and Quidenham in Norfolk, and further afield, Elveden, West Dean, Crichel, Castle Rising, Hall Barn, Welbeck, and a score of others.

There are many accounts of King Edward VII's shooting, and, leav-

ing aside those patriotic writers who averred that he never missed, the general consensus is that he was not as good as some of his subjects. Perhaps Lord Warwick caught the balance best when he wrote, 'If King Edward could not be considered a first class shot, he was at least a good one, and was certainly a first class sportsman.' He was best at driven partridges, least good at pheasants.

As the King grew older, his love of shooting mellowed. It never died, nor even waned, but the occasions on which he went out were fewer. Observers commented on increasing preoccupations which blunted the edge of his skill, and latterly he developed a habit of allowing birds to fly over him without firing. Lord Warwick noticed this one day; noticed, too, that the birds were within his own range. He took advantage of it and had a wonderful drive, shooting not only his own birds, but also those that King Edward did not attempt. At the end of the drive, more as a formality than anything else, Warwick went to the King and said that he might have shot the odd bird which belonged to the King. 'You did, indeed,' was the embarrassing reply, 'but pray don't trouble yourself about it.' After that, any bird that the King chose to leave remained unmolested.

It was very much an age when the Monarch could do no wrong, and such an act was approaching *lèse-majesté*. For all his charm, the King himself was the first to subscribe to this view, and at all sports he liked to excel. This regal attitude showed itself in a game of

King Edward VII.

A game of croquet. This photograph shows a very early houseparty, *circa* 1860.

21

croquet played in Marienbad against Harry Chaplin and Fritz Ponsonby, who tells the story.

'On one occasion at the last moment when someone failed, he asked me to make a fourth at croquet. Croquet is a game the niceties of which I have never mastered, and although I had at various times played, I was a very bad player. To spend hours playing this game did not attract me and I determined to make myself as unpleasant as possible so that I should never be asked again. I drove up with the King to the croquet-ground which was part of the golf club and found that the game had already been arranged, His Majesty and Madame Letellier against old Harry Chaplin and myself. We played for two and a half hours and whenever I got the chance I sent the King's ball to the other end of the ground. This made him quite furious, and the beautiful Madame Letellier who was quite a good player begged me with tears in her eyes not to make him so angry, adding that she understood that courtiers always allowed monarchs to win. I replied that this was out of date and that, personally, I always made a point of beating the Royal Family at any game if I possibly could. I continued my tactics although it made the game distinctly unpleasant. Harry Chaplin, who had played in his youth, seemed to know all about the game and so we went ahead and looked liked winners, but Madame Letellier was too good for us. Just as we were winning she caught us up and made things so awkward that we were held up. Then the King did several hoops and caught us up. We had a very exciting finish and they just won on the post. To my horror the King said that this was by far the best game he had had and that therefore we would have a return match the next day.'

The big shot: the Prince of Wales firing a Maxim gun at Wimbledon, 1888.

Some people behaved better than Lord Warwick and Captain Ponsonby. Most unlikely among them was Lord Rossmore, whose reputation for hard living was well known even in that debauched age. He found himself next to King Edward VII at Elveden when a woodcock suddenly appeared on his left. Thinking that nobody was looking, he stepped smartly to his right, shooed the bird towards the King and shouted 'Woodcock, sir!'; whereupon the King promptly killed it. Someone who noticed this commented afterwards that many a dukedom had been given away for less.

If King Edward VII was not in the top league as a shot, his sons were. Prince Eddie was already a fine shot by the time of his premature death in 1892, but the best royal shot was undoubtedly the second son, later King George V. As a young boy he was very keen, even if unsuccessful at times. Lord Burnham recalls one day when the Prince returned to the house after a day's shooting and explained, 'I can't hit a feather. But I have been at sea for a good many years, and one doesn't see many pheasants there!' By the turn of the century however he was among the six best shots in the country. He had a

Like father, like son : King Edward and the Prince of Wales at Sandringham.

very distinctive technique, with his left arm straight along the barrel, and when he turned to shoot a bird behind him, he would do so with a quick jumpy changing of his feet, which looked unprofessional but was extremely effective. Always with him in later life was his private detective, Mr. Greene, whose job, rather than to protect the King, was to record the number of birds he shot in a drive. This he did with a device which clicked every time it was pressed, and which recorded the total automatically on a dial.

King George V was brought up in a generation when big shoots were the order of the day. He once intimated to a landowner that he would be pleased to accept an invitation pheasant shooting. Unfortunately, it was late in the season and the estate had been heavily shot. The embarrassed peer told the King that they could expect no more than 500 pheasants. 'Never mind,' said the King, 'I should like to come all the same.' The story was told to show how much the King was a man of the people, and though these days that might be stretching credulity, it would be wrong to think of King George V as a man who cared only about the size of the bag. Both he and the Prince of Wales (King Edward VIII) shot with Lord Burnham on the record day in December 1913 when nearly 4,000 pheasants were killed. In the train going home, the Prince of Wales noticed that the King was unusually silent. At last he said quietly, 'Perhaps we overdid it today.'

Lord Burnham counting the bag, Hall Barn.

In the 1850s and early '60s the Prince had been on the lookout for Sandringham.
an estate which he could purchase with his accumulated income from
the Duchy of Cornwall. He looked first at the Lynford estate (later to
become the home of the eccentric Sir James Calder who used to
switch his electric generator off at 10.30 p.m. and plunge all his guests
into darkness). Lynford did not prove suitable, however, and when
Sandringham came on to the market at a price of £220,000, in the
year before his marriage to Princess Alexandra, he bought it. This
estate, with its 8,000 acres spreading over the best game country available, was to become the royal couple's favourite home. An invitation to Sandringham was particularly valued, because it was the
home where Edward entertained his friends. The political houseparties, which might be found at Windsor, or the formal socialising
of London were excluded from Norfolk where the future King was a
country landowner.

The families of Norfolk had always been used to something a little out of the ordinary from Sandringham. It had been owned in the 1830s by a property speculator called John Motteux, at a time when landed estates were the prerogative of the old families, and were rarely regarded as an investment. Although he owned it for a decade, Motteux never lived there. Nothing is known of him except that he was the grandson of the playwright Peter Anthony Motteux, and that he was once involved in a dispute with Lady Holland as to whether prunes should or should not be an ingredient of cock-a-leekie soup. It is not the stuff of which legends are made. His sole contribution to the estate was to plant a considerable number of pear trees in the grounds.

After the pears came the scandal. The Sandringham estate was acquired by the Hon. Spencer Cowper, who married the colourful Countess D'Orsay. Although the lady spent her time in Norfolk immersed in good works, Norfolk was not the place for a girl with a past. She had been the Count D'Orsay's child bride at the age of fifteen, but had spent maturer years in the company of the Duc d'Orléans. After his violent death, she had looked to England. Sandringham was not regarded ideally as a second choice for anyone – at least so thought the Norfolk families.

When the Prince of Wales bought the property, he enlarged and converted the unattractive house that was on the site. It remained a

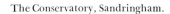

The Conservatory, Sandringham.

house, however, not a palace, and the inside was filled with all the knick-knacks that might be expected in an English gentleman's house of the period. Another cottage was built, at first known as Bachelor's Cottage, when the odious Prince Eddie occupied it to entertain his friends from HMS *Bacchante*, but it was later renamed York Cottage, when the Duke of York had made it his home after he married.

Most of the money spent on the Norfolk estate, and this amounted to £300,000, was spent in transforming it into a world-famous shooting property. The estate was in a part of the country which naturally favoured both pheasants and partridges, but after years of neglect was not in good condition. Lord Walsingham wrote of the Sandringham of the 1860s; 'There was a lot to change – the coverts were scanty, the cultivation poor – the stock of game very limited, and the woods ill-adapted for that system of beating which has become the hall-mark of the well-driven pheasant.' Over the next ten years, under the guidance of Lord Leicester, the Prince set about a systematic transformation. By the turn of the century, the Sandringham estate was rivalled only by Holkham itself.

In one area alone the Prince of Wales was unsuccessful. He tried to widen the variety of the sport by introducing game not indigenous to Norfolk. He first attempted to bring in Virginia quail, which were a partial success in that they were seen to breed – indeed some were

27

shot – but they quickly strayed into the neighbouring countryside. It was as a result of this that a rather puzzled letter appeared in *The Field* of 26 August 1871, in which the writer said that he was almost sure that he had seen a Virginia quail in the area of Thetford, but that he knew he could not possibly have done so. The Editor was able to explain.

The Prince of Wales shared the ambition of so many of the Norfolk landowners in wishing to breed red grouse on his land. Lord Rendlesham had been the first to try in the early 1870s, followed by Duleep Singh and Lord Walsingham, but all attempts failed. The Prince of Wales could reasonably have expected more success on his property, since Wolferton Heath much resembles some of the Yorkshire heathland where grouse are commonplace. The fourteen brace of grouse introduced from Aberdeenshire in 1878/9 did not prove a great benefit to the royal shoot. It was clear by 1881 that at least three brace had bred, and there was evidence as late as 1910 (in the form of

A shooting houseparty at
Sandringham, *circa* 1906.

a solitary feather), that the bridgehead established thirty years earlier
had not entirely passed away. But that was all.

At Sandringham it was the careful treatment of the pheasants and
partridges which made the estate famous. This weight of game was
the envy of the King's other sporting properties, Windsor and Balmoral. The head ghillie at Balmoral wrote to Mr. Willan, who was
living in York House, Sandringham at the time, 'They have a lot of
birds down there in Norfolk.' Anxious to show that Balmoral was
really far superior, he continued, 'I am surprised that you say you
cannot hit the pheasants, as they do not fly in such a hurry as the
grouse.'

There were only two weeks of formal sport at Sandringham each
year. The first of these coincided with the Prince's birthday on
November 9th, and the second with Princess Alexandra's on December 1st. The royal command for these shooting weeks went out well
in advance, so that all who were invited could arrange their other

29

The drawing room,
Sandringham.

engagements accordingly; and also to provide plenty of time for each guest to choose a birthday present for his host (or hostess). The presentation took the form of a little ceremony at which the Prince would express his surprise and pleasure that anybody should have remembered his birthday, and a table was provided on which the presents, usually consisting of gold cigarette holders or similar valuables, would be displayed. On one such occasion, amid the glitter of all the gold and silver, the other guests were amused to see two very dusty and cobwebby bottles of port, bearing a label 'from the Earl and Countess of Leicester'. When the Prince expressed his gratitude for them, Lord Leicester said, 'I noticed that your Royal Highness seemed to enjoy the port at Holkham, so I have brought you two bottles of it.' The general feeling was that he might have made it a dozen!

At the start of the week, the guests would come up from London by train, boarding at St. Pancras Station, and travelling by the special royal train to the Sandringham station at Wolferton, about two miles away. The occupants and their baggage were then transferred to the waiting horse-drawn carriages. The rule that no lady must be seen dressed in the same clothes more than once meant that the amount of luggage taken for a week was phenomenal. As the guests entered the house, their hosts would be there to greet them, but only briefly. The guests would be shown to their rooms, the ladies in the older part of the house, the bachelors in the new wing. And there they would stay; there was no question of midnight liaisons at Sandringham. In their rooms there would be refreshments to revive them from the journey before changing for dinner at eight-thirty – or nine by the Sandringham clocks.

A guest who had not been to Sandringham before might have been surprised to see that none of the clocks showed the right time. Following the example of Lord Leicester, the Prince kept all the clocks running half an hour fast, to get an extra half-hour for shooting on the dark winter days. Some might have thought it easier to start the proceedings half an hour earlier and keep the clocks the same, but Norfolk was a county slow to change, and that applied equally to the starting time for a gentleman's sport.

Entering the dining room was a formal occasion. To avoid any embarrassment of protocol, the Prince quietly told each man whom he was to escort into the meal. The occasion itself was no less formal. The main purpose of the meal was to keep 'Tum-tum' amused. This became increasingly difficult as time went by, and the warning signals of boredom, a drumming of his fingers on the table, or the clattering of his cutlery, did not serve to relax the ladies on either side of him. Lady Fingall admitted that she found it very difficult. 'I never found it easy to amuse him, although he was always very nice to me: "Jolly

Sandringham: the head keeper, Mr. Jackson, and the King outside the luncheon tent.

little lady,'' he used to say, ''jolly little lady,'' when he found my name submitted to him for a party to meet him, and he never scratched my name out.' Alice Keppel, who perhaps knew him as well as anyone, advised those about him to keep talking, as the Prince preferred to listen. 'Often he starts a discussion, but he prefers to listen to theirs: as soon as he can get others involved he is content to listen and make occasional comments.'

Little would be drunk, the Prince himself having only a single glass of wine with his meal, and if he considered that any lady was drinking too readily, the rebuke would rarely be private. Lord Knutsford found the strain of constantly having to do the right thing rather tiring; and in particular the habit of speaking both French and English during the meal, dropping from one to the other in the same sentence.

When at last the meal was over, the ladies retired. The whole tenor of the shooting weeks at Sandringham was much more austere than the parties which happened at other times of the year. Then the glittering ballroom would come into use, and the customary opening quadrille would herald an entertainment which lasted until the small hours. Now it was different. The men would retire to the billiard room for brandy and cigars, and, although they were not allowed to go to bed before their host, Edward did not tend to stay up late. He was very insistent, however, that no one should retire

The squire of Sandringham.

King Edward VII shooting at Sandringham.

King Edward VII at Sandringham: Mr. Robinson, his loader, in kilt.

SANDRINGHAM GAME CARD.

DATE 1905	NO. OF GUNS	BEAT	PHEASANTS	PART-RIDGES	HARES	RABBITS	WOOD-COCK	SNIPE	WILD DUCK	TEAL	PIGEON	VARIOUS	DAILY TOTALS
Nov.7	9	Woodcock Wood	865	1		546	8		275		2	1	1698
.8	9	Flitcham & Appleton Farms	225	655	46	2						1	929
.9	10	Commodore & Dersingham Woods	2728	11	85	23	6				5	1	2859
.10	9	Sherrbourne & Eleven Acres	317	1342	101	5					5		1770
PARTY		WEEKLY TOTALS	4135	2009	232	576	14		275		12	3	7,256

His Majesty The King, Prince Kinsky, The Duke of Alba The Duke of Marlborough, The Earl of Rosebery. Viscount Falmouth Lord Brooke, Lord Lovat, The Hon. G. Keppel, Colonel the Hon. A. E. Legge

The gamecard, Sandringham, 1905. The partridge bag for 10 November was a record for Sandringham.

before him. One evening he walked through the drawing rooms counting the heads, and found one of the guests – as yet unidentified – was missing. A page was sent to find out who it was and fetch him. It turned out to be General Sir Dighton Probyn, VC, then aged seventy-five, who had felt unwell and had gone to bed. He was roused by the page, and brought before the King, who had imagined that it was one of the younger guests. The Monarch was much amused; Sir Dighton was not.

The only diversion was the bowling alley (which was later converted into a library). The Prince was always somewhat reticent about it – perhaps it seemed a little fast. There is a story of a vicar who was staying at Sandringham before going to preach a sermon the following day in the village church. He was induced to retire before the game started, but the next morning at breakfast a fellow guest spoiled the deception by saying to the clergyman, 'You were very lucky to get off so well last night; they got me into the bowling alley and kept me there till 4 a.m.' But, generally speaking, late nights were not the rule, especially if there was to be shooting the following morning.

Breakfast was served at small tables holding six to eight people. None of the Royal Family appeared, which was a relief, and certainly for the ladies it was a very relaxed occasion. The men had to be at their meeting place at the appointed time, when their royal host appeared. There were generally eight to ten guns, each with two loaders.

The first day was customarily spent shooting partridges at Flitcham Farm. Partridges at Sandringham were always particularly successful, under the guiding hand of the head keeper, Mr. Jackson, who went to Baron Hirsch's estate in Hungary to study the best ways of managing them. Sandringham was one of the first estates to employ the remise system, which was designed to concentrate all the partridges into small, twenty-acre areas, to make them easier to drive, since one of the big difficulties with driving large numbers of partridges is that they tend to scatter over a large area. The remise system meant that big bags were much more easily obtained.

The Prince's birthday itself would be the biggest day, and consisted mostly of pheasants driven from Dersingham and Commodore Woods, which contained by far the greater quantity of the ten or twelve thousand birds put down on the estate. (A comparison of these weeks in 1881 and 1905 shows how similar in format these shoots were; the only thing that had changed was that in the later period the bags were bigger.)

By and large, the guns invited to shoot at Sandringham were expected to be good shots. This was not always true of the King's equerries who shot there. Sir Harry Stonor, of course, was one of the best shots in the country, but Sir Charles Cust was no better than average, and Harry Legge, who was out shooting in the 1905 party,

The end of a perfect day, and the end of an era: King Edward VII counts the bag at Sandringham on his 68th, and last, birthday.

can scarcely even be described as that. The Duke of Portland wrote of him: 'He amused me very much, especially one day when we were partridge-driving, because he persisted, against my wishes, in shooting any pheasant that came over; and the excuse he made was "I'm sure you won't mind, old chap, I get so little shooting in the season that I can't help firing at everything I see, by way of practice!" My recollection is, however, that the pheasants suffered very little from his ardour, and the partridges still less!'

It was not possible for all the members of a houseparty to be out shooting at Sandringham, and Edward was always very anxious that his guests should be entertained. It therefore became apparent that if asked by the Prince what you were doing in the morning, it was always wise to have some activity up your sleeve; otherwise you were likely to be organised into some excruciating activity in which you had not the slightest interest. Princess Alexandra would take the ladies around the gardens, and the guests were expected to make admiring noises at all the items they saw, from Sir Harry Keppel's strange Buddhist ornament which he presented to the Prince and Princess of Wales, to the lovely rhododendrons which surrounded the estate.

After the shooting, there was tea in Sandringham House, which was a formal meal and gave the ladies an opportunity to wear their tea-gowns. There was no question of the men who had not shot up to their usual form retiring to their rooms in a huff; all attended, and in the background Gottlieb's band 'played like a bee in a bottle for an hour'. After tea, the avuncular figure of the Prince would preside over games. However, all were expected to remember his position; on one such occasion, after his accession, a friend of the Duchess of Marlborough addressed him as 'my good man', to which he replied, frigidly, 'My dear Mrs. B., please remember that I am not your good man.' Unlike tea, these games were optional, and those who knew the routine tiptoed off to the library to read or talk.

Although it was possible to shoot more birds at Elveden, to shoot better flying birds at Holkham, to have a more riotous time at Chatsworth, an invitation to Sandringham was a royal command which remained, on the whole, a pleasure.

Windsor, the oldest of the King's sporting estates, has a long history. William the Conqueror chose the site of Wyndleshora for a royal seat and he gave its dispossessed owner some land in Essex in exchange. It was selected partly for its 'convenience of hunting', so the history of royal sport at Windsor goes back at least nine centuries. We have a record of George I out pheasant shooting in August, when the birds can scarcely have been able to fly; one imagines that those not killed by the gun would otherwise be picked up by the dogs. It was certainly the place where the Prince Consort enjoyed his pheasant shooting; there is a tree planted at Flemish Farm on the estate to mark the place from which H.R.H. the Prince Consort fired his last shot. Com-

Lord Derby.

The Kaiser at Windsor, 1907.
The Kaiserin preferred to show
her profile and behaved
accordingly.

memorative tree planting was rather the vogue at Windsor; there are
trees to commemorate Edward VII's last shot, George V's first shot as
King of England and several other similar reminders.

Sport at Windsor was never the first love of either King Edward VII
or his elder son. It was much more formal than at Sandringham, as
it was at Windsor that Edward entertained visiting heads of state.
The result was that all court protocol had to be observed: every
activity there was geared to the smooth running of the social and political life which was very much part of Windsor. Just how adroit the
members of the royal household had to be was once shown by Captain
Ponsonby when he was the junior equerry at Windsor. Because the
Spanish Ambassador in England had been accused of attacking the
Spanish government, he had been recalled and was to be replaced by
his chief accuser. The outgoing Ambassador, furious at this indignity,
said that if he ever met his successor he would spit in his face and in-

An early shooting party at Windsor: *left to right* Charles Grey, Major Grey, General Seymour, Prince of Wales, Sir James Clark.

sult him. So when they both came to Windsor, one with a letter of recall and the other with letters of credence, strict instructions were given that they were on no account to meet. Unfortunately the outgoing Ambassador missed his train so he was still in the Castle when his successor arrived. 'I happened to be in the corridor at the time,' wrote Ponsonby, 'and Lord Edward Pelham-Clinton dashed to me and told me to take one of them into a side room and invent any excuse I could think of. I grasped at once what had happened. I seized him by the arm and told him I particularly wished him to see a picture in one of the adjoining rooms. Determined at any price to prevent any spitting, I almost pushed him through the door and shut it. He seemed rather surprised at my haste, but enquired which picture it was I wanted him to see. I pointed to one and said, "We have never been able to find out for certain who it was of and who it was by", But he said "I see clearly the name of Winterhalter on the picture." This was rather a facer for me, but I merely said "Ah, but *is* it by Winterhalter? That is the point!" The poor man was completely puzzled, and proceeded to examine the picture carefully through his glasses. He probably thought I was drunk or mad, but mercifully a page came in and announced that the carriage was ready to take him to the station.'

It was therefore hardly surprising that the shooting at Windsor should be geared to the political rather than the sporting world. Up till the reign of Edward VII, the shooting at Windsor was almost Pickwickian. The Gentlemen of the Household and guests drove from the Castle in a carriage called a sefton which the sentries would always greet by presenting arms to whoever was inside. The head keeper Mr. Overton and all the senior keepers wore green velvet tail coats with gold-laced waistcoats, and when the shoot began, a pack of Clumber Spaniels, considered virtually useless for shooting and then quite out of fashion, would be let loose. The new Monarch gently

King Haakon of Norway's visit to Windsor as it really was.

. . . and as the press saw it.

39

coaxed Windsor out of these archaic practices. Mr. Overton was pensioned off and the job of head keeper was given to one of the Duke of Portland's keepers. He was given a free hand to cut down woods, plant coverts and do what he could to improve the shooting both in quality and quantity at Windsor. This he did very successfully – a little too successfully in fact, as within two years he had to be instructed to make the birds fly lower, since foreign heads of state who were invited to shoot at Windsor were quite often inexperienced at driven pheasant shoots and were unable to cope. On one occasion King George V, when Prince of Wales, killed over 90% of the bag.

Head keeper's cottage, Windsor.

3
The Great Shots

Sir Ralph Payne Gallwey was an outstanding figure of the Edwardian shooting world. His particular love was wildfowling – in the period from spring 1891 to spring 1892 he covered over 7,725 miles in pursuit of it. The perseverance was typical of him, though he is best remembered today for the books on shooting which he wrote at the end of the last century. He collaborated with the late Lord Walsingham, writing a larger proportion in each of the two shooting volumes of the well-known *Badminton Series*. In later life he wrote another outstanding book on shooting and ballistics, *High Pheasants in Theory and Practice*, but perhaps his most characteristic books are the *Letters to Young Shooters* published in a series of three volumes between 1890 and 1896.

The *bon mot* came easily to him. He once occupied a railway carriage with rather an aloof middle-aged lady, and all attempts at conversation having failed, both parties spent most of the journey dozing. When Sir Ralph alighted at his destination, he turned to the lady and said, 'We might not have had much conversation, but at least we can say that we have slept together.' There is another story, too, about his visit to the oculist, when he observed the test card which he knew he would later have to read. He memorised all the letters, and noticed in minute print at the bottom of the right hand corner of the card the words 'McCorquodale and Sons, Printers'. Saying nothing, he waited until the test came, and having correctly identified all the letters he turned to the oculist and said, 'Ah, but I think I can see more than that.' The oculist said that there was nothing else. Sir Ralph, pretending to strain his eyes very hard in the direction of the card, which was at the other end of the room, said, 'You are wrong, I think I can make out the words, "McCorquodale and Sons, Printers" at the bottom right hand corner.' The oculist thought it was a miracle.

In 1886 Sir Ralph moved to Thirkleby Hall near Thirsk. The Hall and the surrounding estate were meticulously maintained and over the years he initiated a number of improvements, including an in-

Sir Ralph at Thirkleby.

door riding stable, private golf links, and an indoor rifle range. He entertained there on a regular basis, and many of the shooting house-parties were attended by the great social names of England. However, the natural eccentricity of the man was always likely to show through. He had, for instance, a passion for ballistics and built great models of the ancient siege engines of early times, with which he would entertain his guests with a display of *ballistae*. This interest in arcane weapons extended to Australian boomerangs and the Sikh quoit, which could be thrown great distances. He was skilled with the cross-

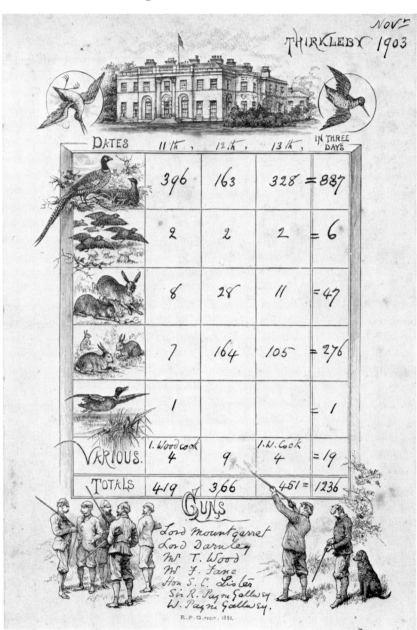

Thirkleby shooting card, designed by Sir Ralph Payne-Gallwey.

The Thirkleby gun room.

bow, and he held the British distance record for archery. He also invented a double-barrelled breech-loading punt gun which was far ahead of anything ever before seen and which was subsequently displayed at the Inventions Exhibition of 1885. His enthusiasm for the sport of shooting was immense: the shooting catalogues of the period bear testimony to his remarkable powers of inventiveness – Payne Gallwey shooting bags, Payne Gallwey gaiters, Payne Gallwey shooting sticks, Payne Gallwey gun cleaning outfits. He died on 24 November 1916 and was laid to rest outside the main entrance of the Chapel at Thirkleby. His grave is inscribed with a short quote from Andrew Marvell: 'He nothing common did, or mean'. It is a fitting epitaph.

Sir Ralph Payne Gallwey with a crossbow of his own invention.

The two people who were without doubt the greatest shots in England were Lord [2nd Marquess of] Ripon and Lord Walsingham. Both by odd coincidence, were known by the name de Grey, though not at the same time: Lord Walsingham, as the Hon. Tommy de Grey, inherited his father's title in 1870, whereas Lord Ripon only became Lord de Grey when his father was created the Marquess of Ripon in June 1871.

Lord Ripon did not inherit many of his father's qualities. The 1st Marquess was Viceroy of India in the 1870s, a statesman of the old school, respected more than he was admired or loved, but a man of unassailable integrity. His only son did stand for Parliament but took

43

Lord de Grey takes a high one.

little interest in the affairs of the House of Commons. Lord Ripon's preoccupation was with shooting, and in a sense he made it his career. Socially, his credentials were impeccable, though – unlike his wife – he could never have been described as good company. His engagement to Gladys Lonsdale had caused something more than surprise. Gladys was one of the fast young ladies so disapproved of by Queen Victoria; her way of life had been summed up by the Prince of Wales's description of her as 'a professional beauty'. Gladys was nothing if not a professional, and following her first husband's death she had been wooed ardently by numerous gentlemen. Why she married the then Lord de Grey is not at all clear. She wrote to Henry Chaplin, one of

44

her admirers, in April 1886: 'I have been laid up with my eyes, or would have written sooner to tell you that I am going to marry Lord de Grey. You are such a true friend that I believe you will really be glad when I tell you that I have at last found peace and comfort, for you know how much trouble I had all my life though I am afraid it was mostly of my own making.' But Gladys preferred power to peace, and marriage to a man who was the heir to a marquessate and 24,000 acres would have some consoling features.

Gladys, who dominated the social scene until her death in 1917, was carefree, musical and frivolous. Her husband (who would ever have called him 'Oliver'?) was austere and humourless. The Duchess of Marlborough remembered: 'Lady de Grey's little informal dinners were invariably gay and amusing ... I recall one at which we were all startled by a frightful clatter of broken china. I was amazed to see the Princess (of Wales) in fits of laughter while Lord de Grey, our host, remained unmoved. It appeared that at a previous dinner, a footman had dropped a tray of Lord de Grey's valuable china; since then the incident had been repeated, with the china specially bought for making a noise.' The couple found themselves at the centre of Society. Gladys provided the fun, and everybody was proud to know the best shot in England. The fact that he was a little single-minded about it did not matter. When everybody else was gambling at Monte Carlo at a time of year when there was no shooting at all, it was Lord de Grey who discovered a cardboard pig shoot at a fair. De Grey was

45

delighted and everybody was expected to go along and try their skill, each shooting with a rifle – except de Grey, who killed all the little piggies with a Mauser pistol.

The legend of Lord Ripon rests simply on the fact that he could kill more birds than anybody else. He himself liked to pretend that his skill was achieved effortlessly, and he once wrote: ' "Practice makes perfect" is in the case of shooting only true to a certain extent, for a man must be born with a certain inherent aptitude to become a really first-rate shot.' In any event it always looks just a little more impressive if success is achieved without really trying. We can therefore forgive Edith Balfour's surprise, when staying at Panshanger. Unable to sleep, she went into the library to take out a book, and there discovered Lord Ripon, attended by his two loaders, practising the art of changing guns. She records that 'he was not too pleased at being discovered'.

In whatever way he achieved it, success certainly came to him; there was nobody his equal. At Sandringham he once killed twenty-eight pheasants in a minute. On another occasion he shot so quickly and accurately that he had seven birds dead in the air at once. His talents aroused some jealousy. Once, while shooting next to a Colonel in Yorkshire, Ripon shot all the Colonel's birds, after the Colonel had

Henry Chaplin.
Lord Ripon's grouse moor at
Studley Royal : the bag.

missed them. At the next drive, an easy partridge flew by, which Lord Ripon missed with both barrels. The Colonel was seen to fall upon his knees exclaiming 'Lord, I thank thee from the bottom of my heart!'

Those who shot with Lord Ripon regularly were anxious to show that they were *nearly* as good – a harmless enough vanity on most occasions, but once it had more serious consequences. His lordship was shooting on the Duke of Cleveland's moor at High Force, and next to him was Lord Wemyss, himself an excellent shot. On this occasion, both were in good form, and a keen rivalry grew up as to who was going to finish the day having killed more grouse. At the last drive of the day, it was Lord Wemyss who drew the better position, and seemed certain of ending up as 'top' gun. Unhappily, as Wemyss was pulling grouse out of the sky, the black powder from his gun (it was before the days of smokeless cartridges) set the butt alight. Lord Wemyss was much too excited to worry about a trifle like that – as he said afterwards, 'Flaming butts do not matter, but to beat the best game shot in England mattered a great deal.' He made no attempt to stamp out the fire, which smouldered in the dry turf until the breeze fanned it into a flame which drove him from the butt. The fire took a fortnight to extinguish, and the entire local workforce had to be employed in carrying buckets of water from the valley below to stop it spreading. Lord Wemyss was happy; his total had topped that of his rival.

Lord de Grey.

Lord Ripon was sensitive about these matters and apparently not averse to a little exaggeration. While staying at Gopsall with Lord Howe an unfortunate incident happened. Lord Ripon had been shooting with Sir John Willoughby's loader and at the end of the day George Howe asked how many birds he had killed. 'A hundred and twenty-four,' he answered, 'and I fired a hundred and twenty-seven cartridges.' Sir John Willoughby was no respecter of persons, and he blurted out, 'That isn't correct, for my servant told me that you fired over a hundred and fifty.' George Cornwallis-West wrote: 'There was a dead silence, broken only by our host hastily rising and suggesting we should join the ladies.'

When asked whom he considered the best shot he had ever seen, Lord Ripon would always reply that it was Lord Walsingham, with regard both to rapidity and accuracy. Lord Walsingham was an altogether more rounded personality than Ripon: unlike his rival, Walsingham had no obvious claims to a position in the Prince of Wales's Marlborough House set. His ancestors had been the squires of Merton, in Norfolk, since the beginning of the eleventh century. It was largely a matter of chance that Tommy de Grey found himself the friend of the Prince of Wales. They were both about the same age; the Prince was born in 1841, Walsingham in 1843. After Sand-

ringham had become the home of the Prince, county life occasion-
ally brought them together. That the acquaintance should develop
into a friendship was due entirely to their common love of shooting.
The Prince of Wales was actively building his Sandringham estate
into a first-class pheasant and partridge shoot, the like of which
England had never seen. On 14 January 1865 the royal couple paid
their first visit to Merton. The first day of their stay was spent hunting, and they got nothing, but the next day was devoted to shooting,
and the result was 514 pheasants, 13 partridges, 35 hares, and 32
rabbits. His Royal Highness was pleased, and it proved to be the first
of many visits.

Unfortunately the Walsingham family could not afford it. It is hard
to think of a man with three estates and over 10,000 acres as the poor
cousin. The 1876 records show that Lord Walsingham had an income
from his Norfolk estates alone of £9,695 a year, and, on the death of
his aunt, Lady Frankland Russell, he inherited two more estates in
Yorkshire. That was at the height of the agricultural boom, however;
later his income started to slip, and the Prince of Wales's set was far
from cheap. (In the 1890s, the Prince took the shooting at Merton, and
in a single year, the wine cellar which had been painstakingly built
up for generations was exhausted.) Walsingham, unlike some of his
friends, had not the weight of income needed. The end was inevitable. In 1912 his indebtedness became apparent, and the Yorkshire
estates were sold. So was the London property which included the site
of the Ritz Hotel, and all the other assets of any value. All that was
left was Merton Hall itself, which could not be sold because it was
subject to an entail. The last seven years of Walsingham's life were
spent abroad.

It would be wrong to think of Lord Walsingham as a snob. He was,
of course, seen at all the smartest shoots in the country; but he went
to them to shoot, not to be seen. When he was not shooting, he was
happiest in the intellectual and scientific world of London, which at
the end of the nineteenth century managed to combine erudition
with a graciousness of living rarely seen in the academic world today.
His particular subject was ornithology, and his knowledge of it was
encyclopaedic. Even in this world, his gun proved useful; all the
humming-birds in the Natural History Museum were shot by Lord
Walsingham, using powder shot so as to preserve the birds from
excessive damage. He was given several academic distinctions; and
in 1879 he was elected to the exclusive Literary Society, the year after
Arthur Balfour, the future Prime Minister. He was made a director
of the British Museum, and was a founder member of the Castle
Museum at Norwich. The Castle Museum did not benefit as much as
the Natural History Museum; their records show that Lord Walsingham gave them a clutch of duck's eggs in 1895.

Curiously enough, comparatively little is known about Walsing-

The 6th Lord Walsingham.

ham's shooting, whereas anecdotes about Lord Ripon's exploits are legion. He apparently showed an interest in pheasants from an early age: there is a delightful entry in the Merton gamebook for 29 December 1852, when Tommy was nine years old. We learn that 'the Hon. Thomas de Grey killed one pheasant (with a stone)'. Underneath Tommy, by then Lord Walsingham, has added 'Roosting on the walnut tree, since blown down, near the back yard gate, Walsingham 1899.'

His record bag of 1,070 grouse which he killed by himself on Bluberhouse Moor on 30 August 1888, is perhaps the most controversial of all shooting records. The moor itself is a remarkable one, in that it is shaped like an hour-glass, and the birds can be concentrated at the narrowest part. It was there that Walsingham's butt was placed and two lines of beaters drove the birds backwards and forwards. The prevailing winds are such that they fly like bullets in one direction, and like owls the other. The record has been criticised as unsporting, but the reason that Lord Walsingham did it was that someone had said that he did not think there were any birds on the moor, and Walsingham wagered that he could kill 1,000 in a day. It has also been suggested that many of the birds picked up were suffering more from exhaustion than gunshot wounds, having been driven so often towards him. Some locals who happened to be bicycling by were said to be amazed to see grouse by the side of the road, too tired to move. There is probably a lot of truth in that. And yet ... King Edward was thrilled when he shot thirty-five on the Sassoons' moor at Tulchan; and Lord Walsingham shot more than a thousand.

It is fitting that the most often told story of sporting skill at the turn of the century concerned both Lord Ripon and Lord Walsingham. The two men were at a pheasant shoot at Lord Ripon's shoot at Studley Royal in Yorkshire, when a covey of eight partridges suddenly swept over a hedge. On seeing the two groups of guns and loaders, the covey scattered in all directions. Both men got a left and right with each gun, so killing the entire covey, which was picked up on the spot. Perhaps most significant is that when Lord Dorchester told the story, it was to show what wonderful harmony of judgment both showed in assessing which birds were theirs.

In 1903 *Bailey's Magazine* published a list of the twelve best game shots in Great Britain. This list was arrived at by an analysis of names sent in by readers of the magazine. The very idea is symptomatic of the age. At the top of the list was Lord de Grey (Lord Ripon), followed by Mr R. H. Rimington Wilson (an odd choice, incidentally: although a first class grouse shot, he was no better than average at pheasants), and Lord Walsingham. Behind him came Harry Stonor, the greatest courtier of his time, and then such names as the Prince of Wales (later King George v), the Maharajah Duleep Singh, Lord Carnarvon, Lord Ashburton and so on.

Sir Harry Stonor at rest (as
Lohengrin), Devonshire House
Ball, 1897.

Sir Harry Stonor at play,
Warter Priory.

The spirit of competition flowed over into the shoots themselves and at Sandringham it was the custom for the equerry to ask each guest at the end of the drive how many birds he had shot. The totals were then read out over lunch, which was splendid for the good shots but less fun for the others. Since only those birds counted that were actually picked, there was a certain amount of gamesmanship after each drive. Lord Ripon remembers an occasion when he was much astonished to see a guest bombarding the butt next to him with dead birds. The neighbour was clearly suspected of having picked up birds that were not his. As Lord Ripon approached he heard the guest shouting as he cast the birds to his neighbour, 'Take the damned lot! I don't care! Take the lot, damn you.' And Lord Rosebery, when invited shooting at Sandringham, and told that he had drawn a position between Lord de Grey and Harry Chaplin, replied that he knew what would happen: that de Grey would shoot all his birds and Harry Chaplin would pick them all up.

There can be little doubt that the extraordinary amount of shooting that was done in England between 1870 and 1914, and the competitive spirit which was fostered between the experts, resulted in a very high standard of shooting indeed. One of the most remarkable features of the period was that the speed with which a man could shoot was valued as highly as his accuracy. De Grey and Walsingham were considered men apart because they could shoot so quickly. When it was said of a shot that he chose his shots carefully, it did not necessarily mean that he was shooting only the easy birds but just that if he was a more experienced shot he could let his gun off more often. This spirit was taken up even by young boys. The young Prince of Wales (later King Edward VIII) wrote to his father in 1912: 'I love shooting more than anything else and it was very kind of you to allow me to shoot so much here while you were away. I have had some splendid practise [sic] and feel that my shooting has much improved. It is the small days that give one far more practise than the big ones. One can takes one's time and shoot much better.'

Yet, even at the turn of the century when the shoots were at their prime, Lord de Grey could write, 'When I am sitting in a tent taking part in a lengthy luncheon of many courses, served by a host of retainers, my memory carries me back to a time many years ago when we worked harder for our sport, and when, seated under a hedge, our mid-day meal consisted of a sandwich, cut by ourselves at the breakfast table in the morning, which we washed down by a pull from a flask; and I am inclined to think that those were better and healthier days. Certainly the young men were keener sportsmen. I remember being hardly able to sleep on the Monday night before a big shoot, and I am sure my feelings were shared by many others of my own age. Now in the youth of the present generation I remark a growing tendency to arrive a day later than they are invited, to be called to London by a pressing engagement the day before the shooting ends, and sometimes even to "chuck" as they euphoniously express it, a visit altogether.'

It was very easy for Lord de Grey to be magnanimous about earlier times. It is the privilege of the professional to pay homage to the amateur, sure in the knowledge that such modesty serves only to highlight the skill of the former. And Lord de Grey was a professional.

4
Famous Shoots

The two men responsible for the science with which driven shooting developed in the 1850s and 1860s were about as different as they could be. Both were aristocrats, both were eccentric, but there the similarities end, apart from the unifying factor of their love of shooting. Elveden, the estate near Thetford, was the home of one of the most prominent and picturesque figures in English society, the

No question of shooting sticks for the bulk of Prince Victor Duleep Singh.

54

Maharajah Duleep Singh. He was the son of the illustrious Ranjit Singh, the one-eyed 'lion' of the Punjab, and of the notorious and beautiful Maharanee Jinda Koür, a woman of remarkable ability and strong will. Duleep lost his throne in his infancy, and came to Suffolk, which he was to make his home for the next thirty years. He was given the rank and precedence of a European prince, retaining his title of Maharajah, and became a great favourite with Queen Victoria. He showed signs of eccentricity at an early age. One day the Queen remonstrated with him because she had been told that he refused to wear woollen underclothing during the winter; and that in spite of his English guardian's repeated entreaties, and the representations made to him of the dangerous English weather, he continued to refuse to do so. 'Ma'am', he replied, 'I cannot wear flannel next to my skin. It makes me long to scratch, and you would not like to see me scratching myself in your presence.' The Queen hurriedly dropped the subject.

As he reached maturity, the pension that he was given by the Government was used to turn Elveden into one of the finest sporting domains of England, and his Perthshire estate of Grandtully was likewise converted into a first-class grouse shoot. (Indeed the record for grouse being shot over a set of dogs was held by the Maharajah shooting on his Grandtully estate.) But in the 1880s financial problems began to overtake him in very much the same way as they later overtook Lord Walsingham. When the Government was unwilling to increase his pension and refused to restore to him the famous Koh-i-noor diamond (confiscated from his family and presented by the East India Company to Queen Victoria*), he left England and set out for India,

A hot corner, Victor Duleep Singh shooting with Lord Carnarvon at Highclere.

* After this incident, the Maharajah, who regarded the diamond as rightfully his, referred to Her Majesty as 'Mrs. Fagin'.

One of Norfolk's Black Princes: Prince Victor Duleep Singh at the Devonshire House Ball.

Holkham Hall.

where he hoped to raise in revolt his old subjects in the Punjab. He was stopped at Aden, where he abjured Christianity and re-embraced the Sikh faith. He then went to Russia in the hope that the government there might champion his cause. The hope was not realised, so he made his home in Paris. A few years before his death in 1893 he expressed deep regret for the hostile attitude he had adopted towards England, and again accepted the pension from the Indian Government. He lies buried in Elveden churchyard close to the graves of his first wife and his children, Prince Freddy and Prince Victor, themselves fine shots in their day and referred to in East Anglia, with refreshing candour, as the Black Princes.

The year after his death, the estate was sold to Lord Iveagh, and the reputation of the Elveden sport continued. Under Tommy Turner, the keeper, the shooting was of a standard similar to both Holkham and Sandringham, and significantly, during the winter months, the system of putting the clocks forward half an hour was adopted there also. By 1914, Elveden had seen as many as 20,000 pheasants reared in a year. After 1914, however, as in so many other places, the decline set in, and apart from exceptional partridge days in the 1920s the bags fell away.

Lord Leicester, another East Anglian landowner, was also a friend of the Prince of Wales. The head of the Coke family, he was the son of the famous 'Coke of Norfolk' who was granted the first earldom of Queen Victoria's reign. A man of immense personality, he had no time for the social life in which most of the other members of the Prince of Wales's set indulged, and his house at Holkham was almost never used for the kind of entertainment which so set the fashion. He himself was a man of austere habits (though he had no less than eighteen children). He had a broad Norfolk accent and he shaved only on Tuesdays and Fridays, when he would take a pony to his barber who lived some four miles away. On one occasion, as an old man, the Earl was due to receive an impromptu visit from Queen Alexandra on a Thursday, and the barber hearing about this suspected that Her Majesty would prefer not to find her host with two days' growth of stubble on his chin. He accordingly arrived at Holkham to shave Lord Leicester, only to be roundly cursed. Surely he knew by now the shaving days were Tuesdays and Fridays? What did he think he was doing coming round uninvited on the Thursday? We have no record of Queen Alexandra's reactions when she arrived.

Lord Leicester was essentially a man of the country. It was probably he more than anybody else who turned the art of driven shooting into a science, and he originated many of the ideas which were used at Sandringham. He is remembered best for his ability to drive pheasants in a method designed to show them to their best advantage. It was said of him, 'No one in England knows better than Lord

Leicester how to make pheasants do what he wants them to. His knowledge of the birds and how to persuade them is so great that it is quite possible that he might be able to achieve what has always been credited to his powers – drive them into his billiard room.'

Holkham was fortunate in that the coverts, which had been planted as early as 1800, were designed with sport in mind; a farsighted act on the part of Lord Leicester's father, and exceptional among landowners of the period. The result was that, by the 1870s, Holkham was already in a position to capitalise on the second Earl's enthusiasm and skill. The estate was surrounded by a continuous belt of trees with the exception of the north-western corner, which was bounded by marshland, and eventually the sea itself. The game was free to roam within the estate but the cloak of trees formed both natural protection for the birds, and a natural boundary beyond which they were reluctant to go.

A detailed record survives of a shooting houseparty staying at Holkham in December 1898, which gives a fair idea of the doyen of the driven shoot itself. The party was a royal one, and included the Duke of York (the future King George V) and his brother-in-law, Prince Adolphus of Teck. The object of the first day was always to drive the pheasants into the south-east corner of Scarborough Wood. Scarborough Wood, and the covert known as Scarborough Clump, was a focal point for the pheasants, being the widest part of the continuous covert. The exercise was extremely difficult, for when a quantity of birds are crammed into a small space, if one pheasant goes wrong and flies away from the guns, it may well cause the others to follow. In addition, with so many birds in so small an area, it was very difficult

Scarborough Clump, 1899: Lord Leicester looks on.

to stop all the birds leaving the covert at the same moment. A burst
of 750 pheasants over the guns may have looked impressive, but not
even a Lord Ripon could have done a great deal about it.

Lord Leicester organised his forces to overcome these difficulties.
The beaters had been up since dawn flanking in the outlying clumps,
and nets were placed across the continuation of the wood to stop the
pheasants running forward further than was intended. The guns as
well as the beaters were part of this manoeuvre. For the entire morning they walked through the woodlands, never being allowed to fire
a shot. At first they were ordered to be silent, then as they approached
Scarborough Wood, told to make plenty of noise to encourage the
birds to run forward. Lunch was the merest concession, and then
came the first and only drive of the day.

And what a drive it was! The guns lined up, three deep, the Duke
of York being one of the guns in the last line. The last line had
particularly difficult shooting as the birds had passed the apex of
their flight, and were beginning to glide downwards. The birds were
put over the guns first by a single keeper flushing them as gradually
as he could out of the clump. After a short while, the keeper was
joined by another, and when the majority of the birds had been put
out in twos or threes, the beaters formed a line and drove out the
whole clump. The bag for the day, which meant in effect that drive,
was over 1,000 head, including 760 pheasants.

With estates like Holkham and Elveden pioneering the new shooting in England, the sport, under the Prince of Wales's influence, assumed new social dimensions. Historically, the great country houses formed centres for the political interests to which their owners subscribed, and an invitation to such a houseparty was only given to those of a similar persuasion. The idea of entertaining men of different political opinion was opened up by the ambitious Lady Waldegrave in her Twickenham house at Strawberry Hill (once Horace Walpole's), but it became much easier when the shooting country houseparty became prevalent. It was, for the first time, possible to use what was essentially a social occasion as an informal forum where politicians could discuss points of view without being observed by the public gaze. Lady Aberdeen, in her delicious *Memories of a Scottish Grannie*, said, 'An informal and pleasant mode of intercourse sprang up which also had important results to the country, for when politicians of different parties were fellow guests under the same roof for a week, differences were apt to be smoothed over, and compromises effected.'

Chatsworth was the house which more than any other helped to lead the way in this revolution. Its owner, the Duke of Devonshire, shocked the social world by inviting Joseph Chamberlain, a man who had made his money in industry and, although a Liberal, represented the radical wing. During the shooting season the royal parties at Chatsworth would be absolutely vast, and, despite its size, the house was at times filled to overflowing. (One is reminded of the plaintive cry of the Grand Duchess of Mecklenburg-Strelitz, on hearing that the Emperor of Austria was coming to stay – 'What are we to do? Our poor palace has only sixty-two bedrooms.') The Duke of Portland records that a friend who arrived late one evening was given a bed in the hall porter's room. He was much amazed when early next morning the letter bags were hurled on top of him, and the postman greeted him with 'Get up you lazy young devil! you've overslept yourself again!' The Duke himself was one of the most extraordinary men of the nineteenth century. For most of his life the 8th Duke of Devonshire bore the courtesy title of Marquess of Hartington, and was universally known as Harty Tarty. His youth had been spent in the company of one of the most successful courtesans of her time, Miss Catherine Walters, known to the world as Skittles. This celebrated liaison provided the Prince of Wales with one of his most famous practical jokes. During an official tour of Coventry an equerry was told to ask the mayor to take the party to a bowling alley as Lord Hartington was especially keen on this game. During the visit Hartington was clearly bored, so the mayor in all innocence exclaimed: 'His Royal Highness asked specially for the inclusion of the alley in the tour in tribute to your lordship's love of skittles.' History does not relate what Lord Hartington said in reply.

In later life, when Skittles had gone, we get a clearer view of this

political sportsman. There were two sides to his personality. The one was of the brilliance of a politician who could make three different speeches with no notes, and indeed no preparation, when he found himself in a tight corner. With this political brilliance went a consciousness of rank. When someone asked him how best to reply to the American greeting 'Pleased to meet you', Lord Hartington replied, 'I should say "And so you damn well ought to be!"' He married a German known as the Double Duchess Louisa (previously Duchess of Manchester), and the social as well as the political world bowed before them. The Devonshire House Ball, given in 1897, was probably the single most important social event of the generation.

The other side of the Duke's personality was that of a charming buffoon. Always appallingly dressed, his *bête-noire* was the wearing of Orders and decorations. King Edward VII on one occasion begged him not to wear the Order of the Garter upside down. When the

Chatsworth.

61

Harty Tarty with rumpled hose at the ball he gave at Devonshire House, 1897.

King of Portugal presented him with the high Portuguese Order of the Tower and the Sword, the Duke was not the slightest bit impressed. He wore it to dinner, and afterwards, when playing bridge, held one bad hand after another. At last he said, 'I believe that damned Elephant and Castle is bringing me bad luck. If I have another bad hand I will throw the wretched thing into the fire.' The Marquis de Soveral, then Portuguese Minister to this country, had the good grace to join in the laughter.

The Duke suffered, too, from a constitutional sleepiness. When asked why he spoke so seldom in the Upper House, he replied, 'I can't refrain from yawning in the middle of my rare orations. Indeed,

I fell asleep one afternoon and dreamt that I was addressing that just assembly, and when someone woke me up, I found that my dream was true. I *was* speaking to their Lordships.' He was seen asleep in the House of Lords and when he woke, he looked at the clock and said, 'Good heavens, what a bore! I shan't be in bed for another seven hours!'

This mixture of muddled majesty permeated the shooting parties themselves. In 1907 the King and Queen stayed at Chatsworth for a very impressive week's shooting. 'Everything was managed in a most princely way, and the dinners were a wonderful sight. All the women wore tiaras and jewels, while the men wore Orders and decorations. While everything was beautifully managed, anything that was left to the Duke to decide was invariably forgotten. For instance, with so large a party it was impossible for all the men to shoot, and yet the Duke never selected the guns until very late at night, and so the list was only made known during the next morning. Lord Rosebery, who was staying there, once came down to breakfast in shooting clothes, when he happened to meet his valet, who said, "You had better take those clothes off, my lord, as you are not on the shooting list." Rosebery was furious, and immediately left for London. No one also could discover the principle on which the guns were chosen, because there

Houseparty at Chatsworth, January 1907.

was no principle. If the Duke happened to be sleepy he simply said the same guns as before so that men who had been left out the first day, and imagined they would have their turn, found themselves again omitted on the second day.'

Despite the fact that the Duke of Devonshire owned one of the finest shooting estates in England, he was an indifferent shot. His friends were therefore surprised when shooting at Creswell Crags, as Lord Hartington, he killed an exceptionally high flying partridge with a clean kill. His friends thereupon gave a loud cheer. When the drive was over, Hartington asked, 'I wonder why Harry Chaplin and the others cheered when I fired both barrels at a cock pheasant and missed?'. When it was pointed out to him that he had killed the highest partridge of the day, Hartington replied, 'Did I? I didn't even know it was there. However, it's over now, so don't say anything about it, and let me keep my reputation.' So much for the secrecy of his friends; the place was immediately named Hartington's Stand.

One particularly unfortunate shot fired by the Duke of Devonshire was at a wounded cock pheasant as it passed a gate. He fired at it and killed it, and also a retriever which was running after it. With the same shot he hit the owner of the retriever in the leg, and the chef from Chatsworth, who was an onlooker. The Duke was very concerned about this – but only because, all the dinners might have been spoiled had the chef been badly wounded.

The position of Blenheim was very similar to that of Chatsworth, although its owner, the Duke of Marlborough, was less eccentric

Blenheim Palace.

than the head of the Cavendish family. Lord Randolph Churchill,
younger brother of the 8th Duke, was the political force in the family,
and a very considerable one. He was not, however, the most tactful of
men. One day, while shooting at Wynyard, he had the misfortune to
shoot a pet dachshund belonging to a lady of quality. She was very
upset, and Lord Randolph determined to put the matter right. He
had the dachshund stuffed and mounted in a glass case, and gave
it to her as a Christmas present. The result was not very successful,
and caused the lady floods of tears.

The shooting houseparties at Blenheim had by the 1890s become
as splendid and influential as at Chatsworth. In 1896 the Prince of
Wales expressed a wish to come to shoot there and his arrival for a
shooting party in the autumn of that year marked a social high
point at Blenheim. Many of the political leaders of the time were
there: Arthur Balfour, later Prime Minister, wrote of the week:
'There is here a big party in a big house in a big park beside a big
lake. To begin with (as our Toast lists have it) "the Prince of Wales
and the rest of the Royal Family –" or if not quite that, at least a
quorum, namely himself, his wife, two daughters and a son-in-law.
There are two sets of George Curzons, the Londonderrys, Grenfells,
Gosfords, H. Chaplin, etc., etc. We came down by special train –
rather cross most of us – were received with illuminations, guards of
honour, cheering and other follies, went through agonies about our
luggage, but finally settled down placidly enough.

'Today the men shot and the woman dawdled. As I detest both
occupations equally, I stayed in my room until one o'clock and then
went exploring on my bike, joining everybody at luncheon. Then,
after the inevitable photograph, I again betook myself to my faithful
machine and here I am writing to you. So far you perceive the duties
of society are weighing lightly upon me.'

65

The shooting itself at Blenheim was good enough to attract the regulars: de Grey, the young Duleep Singhs, and Harry Stonor. It was, however, no better than that, except for the rabbits, and Blenheim holds the record for the number of rabbits killed on a single day in England: nearly 7,000.

The political example of Chatsworth and Blenheim was not followed by the Londonderrys at their Durham home of Wynyard Park. Wynyard Park remained a bastion of Conservatism, and there was no question of any parleying with the opposition. The guest lists were nevertheless resounding. In October 1903 the Londonderrys had invited a houseparty to Wynyard which included King Edward VII. On the first evening some important diplomatic business arose which had to be dealt with promptly. The King decided to hold a Council there and then. The last sovereign to hold a Council outside a royal palace had been King Charles II, but such was the strength of the guest list that a quorum of Privy Councillors was easily found and the Council was convened.

In London, Londonderry House was the rallying point of all Conservatism. Indeed, when Herr Lichnowsky, the German Ambassador, gave a first official dinner at the German Embassy, Lord Londonderry was present. When the doors opened, and the Liberal Prime Minister Mr. Asquith was announced, Lord Londonderry gave a snort of indig-

Lord Albemarle starting a drive at Quidenham.

nation and, his face crimson with rage, announced that he was leaving, since the Ambassador had insulted him in asking him to meet Mr. Asquith. It was only with great difficulty that he was persuaded to stay.

There were many other shooting estates also, each with its own distinctive personality, and the fact that the owners were not always of the oldest and most noble families was no bar to the entertainment that could be provided. The two English estates which vied for the record pheasant bag, Lord Nunburnholme's Warter Priory and Lord Burnham's Hall Barn, were both owned by men who had been given peerages rather than inherited them.

The Nunburnholmes' shoot at Warter was possibly the most famous of all. The Golden Valley drive was unparalleled for both quantity and quality of birds. Mrs. Hwfa Williams wrote in her memoirs: 'I remember at one stand over 1,500 head of pheasants were killed. Lord Howe, Lord Ripon, Harry Stonor, Bertie Willoughby [Lord Willoughby de Eresby] and Bertie Tempest [Lord Bertie Vane-Tempest] were at this stand; the birds were flying very high and it was really most tiring work to shoot them, but with four guns apiece they brought down this enormous bag. Naturally in these conditions, especially with the birds flying so high, the men were tired out when they came back. Unfortunately, Bertie Tempest used to get terrible headaches after the high stands at Warter.'

Not far from Warter Priory was Lord Savile's estate at Rufford,

67

Lord Alington at Crichel.

Lord Bertie Vane-Tempest
earning a headache.

and Lord Ripon's own shoot at Studley Royal, where the high pheasants flew over a valley, and if they were higher than the tops of the ruins of Fountains Abbey, you left them; they were out of shot. Another well-known pheasant shoot was at Panshanger, the home, after 1905, of Lord Desborough, father of Julian Grenfell. Lord Desborough himself was an all-round sportsman. Perhaps his most remarkable feat was to swim the Niagara pool as near as possible to the Falls in 1884, and when, four years later, an American expressed 'surprise, amounting almost to doubt' concerning this achievement, he did it again. Ettie, his wife, was furious.

There were great partridge shoots as well. One of the best was Lord Ashburton's at The Grange, Alresford, in Hampshire, but it was generally the Norfolk and Suffolk estates, notably those of Lords Henniker, Huntingfield and Albemarle which provided the best partridge days. The Prince of Wales shot with Lord Albemarle first at Quidenham in 1897, and returned there when he became King, but Albemarle's coolness for the behaviour of his sister-in-law, Alice Keppel, stopped the visits being as regular as they otherwise might have been.

Where there's mustard, there's money: Mr. Russell Colman's Norwich shoot, 1910.

5
The Foreigner as Host & Guest

La maladie anglaise: The Parisian view of driven shooting – Anna Tariol-Baugé at the Théâtre des Variétés.

Particularly in his earlier career, the Prince of Wales shot in several different parts of the world. As a young man of twenty-four, he had had experience of a few days shooting in Albania (curtailed by fears of revolution) and some less precarious sport in the Near East. A few years later he went to India – in those days the sportsman's paradise. Life moved slowly, and for those with the time and inclination both big-game and shotgun shooting were richly available. It was an Indian nobleman, the Dewan of Vizianagram who, when some visitor had complained of a lack of game, addressed a subordinate with the words: 'How, Amildar! No tigers for gentlemen! What administration is this?' The Prince's experience in India was mostly of the big-game variety, and it was left to other countries to provide the more exotic shotgun forays which were more to his taste. In Egypt he blasted twenty-eight flamingoes out of the morning flight before tackling bats in the tomb of Rameses IV. The bag this time was only one – to the Prince's gun – but at least everyone (except possibly the archaeologists) was pleased with the story.

As the Prince matured, the attraction increasingly became the Middle European estates, with their phenomenal concentrations of partridges and hares – the estates of Count Trautmansdorff in Bohemia, and those of the Karolyis and Hirsch in Hungary. The development of these estates was in many ways even more remarkable than what was being done in England. Although Europe had known the *battue* long before England, its refinement had been left to the English landowners. The French-speaking world was hesitant about driving game, and although today the driven partridge in Spain is one of the most exciting experiences in shooting, it was then almost unknown. King Alfonso XIII of Spain was so impressed by the driven sport he saw at Windsor, that he determined to copy it. He hired an Englishman by the name of Watts, who, along with two thousand pheasants' eggs and some red-legged partridges, came to the King's private estate at Casa de Campo and organised a *battue* in the English style.

England however was the pupil rather than the teacher of the techniques Baron Hirsch employed at St. Johann and Eichhorn. The Sandringham game-larder was based on that of St. Johann and with a capacity of 7,000 was – after St. Johann – the biggest in the world. The remise system of rearing partridges at Sandringham was also a Hungarian idea, and when the stocks of partridges fell drastically in the late 1870s it was with Hungarian stock, caught in nets and sent to this country, that the numbers were augmented.

Not every idea was followed. The Bohemian band, for instance, which forlornly accompanied lunch, seemed to some more of an embarrassment than a pleasure, and at Sandringham and on other English estates this musical backup never caught on. The countryside, too, with its wide hedgeless spaces and maize which grew in strips, was very different from the English scene, and so the methods of driving were different. It was not unusual for the guns to walk with the beaters rather in front of them, to take advantage of the open stubble which separated the strips of maize. But a description of the sport makes it clear why the Prince of Wales was so enthusiastic.

'The clouds of partridges which come out of each strip are absolutely bewildering. At first, before any birds have been scattered, coveys come out four and five at a time, and get packed like grouse. All these birds rising close round the guns, together with swarms

71

The Emperor Franz Joseph of Austria.

of hares, which jump up in every direction, present the most extra-ordinary sight as they go streaming across the open stubble, and the shooting is pretty lively all along the line until the arrival of the beaters into the open space, when there is a brief halt to pick up the birds. A few small boys follow each gun, and it is their particular duty to collect and carry what falls to the gun of each shooter they follow. Undoubtedly, to judge from the zeal which these urchins display in trying to claim every bird which they can see, they make small wagers amongst themselves on the results of the pickup during the day that is accredited to their respective masters. Retrievers are not often used, and consequently many runners are lost in the high maize; but it would be hard to prevent any dog from flushing scores of birds

72

if put on a running partridge only a few yards in front of the line. With the exception of one or two dogs used by the headkeepers behind the line, retrievers are hardly in evidence at all.'

The hare shooting was equally remarkable. No hares were shot at all until November, when an army of beaters, 600 strong, would form a hollow square and drive the game towards the waiting guns. There was a plentiful supply, too, of pheasants, which rarely had to be fed by the landowner, as the growing maize provided all their needs. Only after the harvest was any feed left for the birds; all the birds were wild, none were reared. It is hard to focus on the size of some of the bags: on Baron Hirsch's St. Johann estate in 1892, 17,048 partridges were killed – the best day on the estate being 2,870 birds. Lord Ripon once killed 7,000 partridges to his own gun during a five week stay as the Baron's guest. On the 10 December 1909, 6,125 pheasants were killed on Count Louis Karolyi's estate at Totmagyar, in north-west Hungary; and in 1894 Hirsch's shooting party bagged 7,500 hares and 2,500 partridges in six days. The English were regular guests: Baron Hirsch's Jewish origins, apparently an obstacle to some of the Austrian and Hungarian nobility, were certainly not going to stand in the way of sport like this.

As well as in Hungary, the partridge flourished in Germany, although Edward's experience of shooting there had its vicissitudes. It was the custom, which increased in regularity as time went on, for him to retire to one of the spas to take the cure, and lose a little weight. This was a regular feature of society, and there were several such spas in Germany – at Baden-Baden, for instance and Schwalbach. Daisy Fingall has given us a charming picture of the seriousness with which the health cure was taken: 'From London I went with Mrs. Willie Jameson to Schwalbach to take the sulphur baths – a delightful place where you had all your meals out of doors among the flowers and the fountains. Although we were supposed to be doing the cure, the food was delicious ... When anybody wanted to pay you a compliment as a gallant friend of mine did, they offered you a rose bath. For this, the petals would have been picked from hundreds of roses and strewn on top of the glutinous water. You lay in your bath with water up to your chin and presently a tray was laid across the bath in which was placed a cup of delicious chocolate and brioches for your enjoyment.'

But it was to Marienbad that the royal party went every year – perhaps the King did not like rose petal baths. Neither his contempt for his cousin, the Kaiser, nor the amazing prices could stop him going. Of course, it was his entourage rather than himself who bore the brunt of the inconvenience. Fritz Ponsonby, the equerry who often accompanied him, wrote:

'Life at Marienbad was very hard work, as I spent so much time seeing people who were difficult to get rid of. For instance, one day

Archduke Franz Ferdinand.

I saw an Austrian Countess who wanted to take her dogs to England, and thought I could give them a pass to prevent them going into quarantine. She was followed by an American who had some place in Austria; other visitors were an officer who had invented a scabbard which telescoped up when the sword was drawn, a sculptor who wanted to do a bust of the King, and a beautiful woman from the half-world of Vienna who wanted to have the honour of sleeping with the King. On being told that this was out of the question, she said if it came to the worst she would sleep with me, so that she would not waste the money spent on her ticket; but I told her to look elsewhere for a bed.'

One of the difficulties to which Fritz Ponsonby refers was the Abbot of Tepl. His Order owned not only the spa and baths at Marienbad, but much of the land surrounding the town, and his duty was to manage the vast properties belonging to the monastery. He spent much time pestering Ponsonby for advice on how to attract more

Fritz Ponsonby and his wife shooting at Combe Abbey (Lord Craven's) 1910.

English people to Marienbad. The King, as he now was, was comparatively easy to lure: the Abbot organised a partridge shoot. Despite the natural abundance of game, nothing like it had ever been seen before. Indeed more partridges were imported by train for the occasion. The performance began with a gargantuan lunch in the refectory of the monastery, at which all the King's party, including the ladies, were present. So long was the bill of fare that it was well past two in the afternoon before the guns were placed. The Abbot had had butts specially constructed and it was evident that the services of the whole population of the neighbourhood for miles around had been requisitioned. Those employed as drivers and flankers were under the immediate command of some of the more venerable members of the fraternity; those who came as spectators unfortunately wandered about wherever their fancy took them. One old monk came out with an old-fashioned gun and a bag of cartridges. This alarmed Eddy Stonor, who asked him where he intended to go. The monk replied that he was going by himself behind the beaters, and added, 'It will all be quite safe, but of course if anyone shoots at me, I will shoot back.' The Abbot himself, in a very short shooting-coat over his white cassock, and a rather *avant garde* hat, moved into position behind the King's butt and lit up a large cigar. When all was in place a horn sounded and the fun began. Two gigantic kites were launched (not one of the ideas borrowed from Baron Hirsch) with the object, it later transpired, of concentrating the birds, and driving them over the King's butt, which for some mysterious reason was placed on the right wing. The partridges reacted unhelpfully and instead of taking to the air, ran along the ground, mingling with the crowd of sight-seers and assorted well-wishers. Those few which did fly over the guns were rarely fired at, for fear of hitting a spectator. Fritz Ponsonby was instructed to find out the total bag for the day, which was thirty-six brace, 'but later I found that the ranger had counted all the birds that had died in the train or been knocked on the heads by the beaters, so eventually a game card was framed showing that the bag was 150 brace.' If it was not a day of which all sportsmen could be proud, at least the Abbot received his reward: not very long afterwards he was invited to Windsor, and was shown round the castle and its treasures by the King himself.

Away from the great partridge and hare shoots of Hungary and Bohemia, there was the much less sophisticated sport to be found in Mediterranean. This was essentially young man's sport. For one thing there simply was not the weight of game to be found in this part of the world: a few snipe and quail, and at times a great many duck in the wide blue bays. But the shooting approximated much more nearly to the French word 'la chasse', for every bird killed usually meant several miles' walk. Here is a description of such sport in Syracuse in the late 1880s:

Puccini duck shooting at Torre
del Lago. His black labrador,
Scarpia, is not present.

76

The guide offered to show us sport 'una chasse incroyable questa sport magnifiquo'. Punctually at 11.30 we started off and after about three quarters of an hour alternately rowing and pushing the boat up the river, we arrived at the marsh and landed or rather disembarked out of a dry boat into water above one's knees. 'Too wet for snipe' said I, but the guide would not have it, and he was right, for 100 yards further on they began getting up like sparrows out of the tufts of reeds. And, O, those reeds! Strong as porcupine quills and sharp as needles. Nothing was proof against them. A quarter to half an hour shooting in this stuff, with three and a half couple, was enough. Every time we fired at a snipe, out of the marshes we would get a whole flock of duck, which, after wheeling once round, pitched again almost in the same place. We went after them; deeper grew the water, till it was well up over our waist, and then it shallowed. A few steps further, up got the duck, bang went six barrels and down came four dead as mutton. 'Good sport! Let's pick up the birds.' Shoulder to shoulder we marched, a stagger and souse we all went head over heels into some twenty feet of water.

A certain Mr. Bagot wrote a guide to the sport in 1887 and he captures the atmosphere perfectly. 'What does one need for such an expedition? A good service revolver and a fairly large hunting knife, being handy as a last resort in case of Piggy charging home. A water bottle covered with felt of the service pattern in which can be carried either water or claret is also a good thing – in fact I would recommend two or three.' These jaunts, which could last for anything up to six months, were very much the activity of the younger sons of England, who had nothing better to do with their time. One could stop off at Cannes and catch up on the expatriate English and then pass further east for the sport. Here we meet a marvellous collage of the ridiculous and the sublime. Bagot tells of the local guides' 'welcome my lords' – everybody was 'my lord' to an excited local, especially with the bevy of natives all begging for *bashuti* (gun-powder). The biggest problem of all were the dogs, which were savage brutes. Bagot was convinced that if one of these dogs were killed or injured even in self-defence, its Albanian master would think no more of putting his long knife into you than hacking off the bough of a tree. But an English naval captain did not find this too much trouble when he was shooting in Montenegro between the wars. He was a man of immense power, and was attacked by an alsatian in the wild mountain regions. He caught the dog in mid-air, and with one wrench broke the beast's back in two. The astonished owner was so impressed with this feat that he presented the captain with a brightly ornamented dagger with which he was armed. The captain discovered later from a shop in Bond Street that it was one of three specially made for the King of Greece. Nobody knows how it got into the dog-owner's possession.

Foreigners who came to shoot in England could not always be relied upon to conform with the general patterns of behaviour. For every individual guest invited because of his love of shooting, there were probably five who came for reasons quite unconnected with the sport.

A Swedish peasant.

77

The problem showed itself early. Lord Tennyson in the 1850s invited a Russian nobleman to his home on the Isle of Wight, and used to send him off with a gun in the mornings to walk the hedgerows. One day the Russian came back looking pleased with himself and reported in a thick Slav accent that he had shot two peasants. Tennyson corrected him, saying 'two pheasants.' 'No,' said the Count, 'two peasants. They were insolent, so I shot them.' It was a situation echoed fifty years later, when an Englishman shooting in Sweden refrained from firing at a hare because there was a beater in the way. His host afterwards chided him, saying 'In Sweden we have many peasants, but not many hares.'

This cheapness of human life was a trait which Lady Cardigan emphasised in her vitriolic memoirs, written in old age and castigating all except Lord Cardigan. She married, after years of widowhood, a Portuguese gentleman, the Count of Lancastre, who used to bring his cronies to England for the pheasant shooting. 'We filled all their cartridges with bran, we were so frightened,' she wrote. She does not tell about the time that her first husband once accused his keeper of extravagance in using men instead of boys for flankers, to be met with the withering retort, 'Beg pardon, my lord, but your lordship will remember that last year you shot down all the boys.' It was generally true that such damage was unintentional, although it cannot have been much of a comfort to know that death had been due to incompetence rather than malice.

An eminent foreigner who was not a safe shot could be a severe embarrassment for the host. Few can have been tactful as Lord Pembroke when faced with such a situation. There was a houseparty at Wilton House in the early 1870s and among the guests was the Ambassador of a European power. During the first day's shooting he had managed to hit, as well as a few pheasants, a number of beaters, keepers, and guests. Those who survived were badly frightened. Lord Pembroke was determined that the man should not be allowed out again. His chance came just before the assembled guests went into dinner, when the Ambassador noticed a great bustard in a glass case. The bird, shot in Wiltshire over sixty years earlier, was the last local example of the species to have been seen. Lord Pembroke inquired whether His Excellency would like to try for one the following day. So, as the main shooting party continued their sport, the Ambassador, balanced on a pack pony, set off towards Salisbury Plain.

King Edward VII had a different method. If he was not sure about the skill of one of his guests, an equerry was detailed off to take the stand next to the gun. When Monsieur Poklewski-Koziell, First Secretary of the Russian Embassy, was shooting at Balmoral in October 1906 it was Captain Ponsonby who was put next to him. Ponsonby related: 'I didn't care much about this as, if he was not a safe shot, I should only find this out by being peppered. It reminded me of a

King Carlos' successor, Manoel II of Portugal, driving to the butts with Lord Ripon at Studley Royal, 1911.

Shah of Persia who on a visit to England was shown the gallows, which interested him very much. He asked whether he could see them in use but the Governor of the gaol said that unfortunately they had no one who was to be hanged. "That is all right. Take one of my suite!" exclaimed the Shah.' In fact the Russian proved to be quite a good shot – unlike another foreigner out grouse shooting in Scotland whose host had gone up to him at the end of a drive to ask him how he had got on, and had been told that he had been unable to hit any of the furry little birds, but of the 'moutons sauvages' he had been able to shoot three.

Some of the foreigners were distinguished shots. One of these was the Archduke Franz Ferdinand, and when he got used to the high pheasants which were not usual in Austria, he performed very well indeed. His death in Sarajevo in 1914 was the spark which ignited the First World War. In fact, when the Archduke was staying at Welbeck the previous December he had a narrow escape. There was rather deep snow on the ground, and during a drive one of the loaders fell down. Both barrels of the gun he was holding went off, and the shot passed within a few feet of the Archduke. One wonders whether the near miss was historically inconvenient.

Another very fine shot was fat little King Carlos of Portugal, assassinated in 1908. He loved to be best at whatever he was doing, and whenever a sycophantic courtier told him that he was good at billiards or painting or whatever, he would proudly tell everyone he met of his reputation. He shot regularly at Windsor, and Elveden, and if he thought anybody was looking, would shoot from both shoulders alternately, then, taking the gun in one hand like a pistol, he would shoot low pheasants holding the gun outstretched in front of him.

King Alfonso XIII as guest of the
Duke of Sutherland, in his own
version of plus-fours.

The Spanish King, Alfonso XIII, who had survived an assassination attempt on his wedding day in 1906, came to England that year, and startled everybody by winning the Isle of Wight clay pigeon trophy. He then proved his skill at Windsor, and then also in Scotland, shooting grouse as the guest of the Duke of Sutherland.

These three were the monarchs who shot most regularly in England. In addition the German Emperor was also a regular shot in England. Although the German press provided impressive statistics of his shooting prowess and he came to England with a great reputation as a shot, he was little more than average. This was hardly surprising as his withered arm meant that he had to shoot with a 20-bore, which lessened his range and effectiveness. He shot grouse regularly with Lord Lonsdale at Lowther. Someone taunted Lord Lonsdale about this friendship during the First World War, to which he replied, 'Well! it only shows how careful one should be about picking up acquaintances when abroad.' Less attractive than the Kaiser himself were his suite. Having no knowledge of the sport, many of them behaved very badly, and when one killed a pheasant at a range of 120 yards, it was discovered that he had been shooting with a small-bore rifle, with a range probably approaching one mile. Nobody liked to say that the entire team had been in danger of their lives for most of the day, as this might have provoked a diplomatic incident. But it meant that those who engaged in the sport at Windsor were chary about the skill of their neighbours, and accordingly, the place was perhaps never as popular as it might have been.

6
Proprieties and Improprieties

The Marquis de Soveral being exquisite.

The shooting weeks which were so much enjoyed by the gentlemen were of less interest to the ladies. There was little to do indoors. The men had breakfasted early and taken to the field by the time the ladies appeared, and the main female amusements were restricted to talking to each other or writing letters. It was sometimes slightly difficult to know to whom one should write – a little silly to choose one's husband, only two fields distant, banging away at the pheasants; so it was small wonder that Harry Cust and others like him were in receipt of so many *billets-doux*. Here is one written to Joe Laycock by Daisy Brooke, in which the start of the grouse season on August 12th is anticipated with considerable gloom: 'I send you this letter, my Joe, by messenger boy as I don't know how posts go about a camp . . . if you are free from drills in the afternoon (as a Major I suppose you are fairly free?) perhaps an afternoon would be possible? Could I give you a picnic dinner here? Brookie will be back on August 6th and off shooting on 12th – but so will Joe. No women exist – wives or mistresses – after August 12th.'

The more thoughtful hosts invited gentlemen who showed no talent for shooting, but whose wit made up for it. These 'darlings' were usually drawn from court circles, and one of the best of them was the Portuguese minister in England, the Marquis de Soveral. Despite an unprepossessing exterior (he was fondly known as the Blue Monkey), he had that rare talent of keeping people amused – even King Edward VII, when the strain of office and bronchial troubles made him progressively more difficult to please. It was clear, too, that Queen Alexandra found de Soveral enjoyable company. He was a wonderful raconteur – to the point, sometimes, of monopolising the conversation. On one occasion Prince Francis of Teck remarked to him: 'My dear Soveral, would you mind if I slipped a word in every five minutes, and a phrase every half hour?' Daisy Princess of Pless points to a similar trait. Staying at a houseparty at Chatsworth in 1907, she wrote: 'Only Soveral was furious; he was rather the odd man out, which as a rule he never is.'

The shooting lunch was an important feature, and many of the
hosts went to elaborate lengths to make it memorable. There were, of
course problems – the guns might be some distance from the house
at lunchtime and it was difficult, too, to ensure that the last drive
before lunch finished at the appointed time. But there were some epic
feats of administration. At Hall Barn, Buckinghamshire, on the day
in December 1913 when the record bag of 3,937 pheasants was shot,
lunch was on a scale similar to the shooting. The host, Lord Burnham,
provided an enormous marquee. The guns were joined by twenty
guests who had been invited especially for the lunch. Although it
lasted only an hour and a half, it was a meal of five courses, and the
Prince of Wales remembered the majordomo being caught out by one
of the more abstemious guests who asked, unsuccessfully, for a glass of
iced water.

On the days when King Edward VII was shooting, the menu for
lunch was always chosen with him in mind, for it was known that
'Tum-tum' enjoyed his food. The Hall Barn lunches would have an
oyster course of which the King was very fond; indeed it was Lord
Burnham who had organized the Oyster Banquets for His Majesty
in London. These were banquets for hundreds of people, the King
being the guest of honour. Through these it became well known that

83

the King enjoyed shell fish, but there were pitfalls even for a shooting lunch. Lady Cadogan was somewhat discomforted when her royal guest started to spit the crayfish on to his plate; he was apparently worried about fish-poisoning. This in turn so flustered Lady Fingall, sitting next to the King, that she nervously addressed him as Sir Ernest for the rest of the meal. The German-born financier, Sir Ernest Cassel, who was sitting on her left, was correspondingly upgraded to the rank of King.

The wine was always of the best. The King drank only Château Lafite whenever he drank claret, but for much of his life champagne was the only alcohol he took. He was particularly fond of old vintage champagne. On very hot days he would drink lemon squash, a drink that owed its popularity to its royal patronage. Both King Edward and Queen Alexandra tended to disapprove of spirits being drunk

at lunchtime; but if the King had been shooting badly and needed a restorer, he would on rare occasions have a cocktail of his own invention.

The dangers of such a good meal in the middle of the day were clear, and at times the standard of shooting after lunch could not compare with the morning's performance. At the beginning of the nineteenth century, it was not usual for a team of guns to shoot for a full day, so the problems arising from a shooting lunch did not arise. (Lord Warwick thought that the 'modern tendency to serve a miniature banquet at one o-clock would have provoked our fathers to laughter.') At Windsor, when the Prince Consort was alive, there was a rule that nobody might shoot after lunch. This rule was continued by Queen Victoria in memory of her husband, and by the time she died in 1901, the rule was hopelessly anachronistic. There was, how-

Lunch at Quidenham. Lord Albemarle retains his horn.

Lunch at Holkham.

ever, no gainsaying a royal command, and consequently there was an arrangement whereby lunch was delayed until 3 p.m., and was brought out to the guns. It was not the ideal way to enjoy the shooting, but at least it meant that the guests received nearly a full day in the field.

The lunch at Holkham was possibly the worst. Lord Leicester regarded the day's sport at Holkham as an exercise in which the guns were expected to play a major role. On the first day's shooting at Holkham, lunchtime would occur while the pheasants were being walked towards Scarborough Clump. The serious business took priority, and lunch was a pretty Spartan affair. Talking was discouraged, as it might disturb the birds. One was allowed to sit down if one wanted, though it was not recommended, and the meal itself consisted of a few sandwiches hastily swallowed, and nothing to drink at all unless someone had the forethought to bring some brandy in a flask. There was no question here of being joined by the ladies. It says a good deal for the quality of the shooting at Holkham that it was the place to which every shot in England wanted to be invited.

At Sandringham, too, it was customary to have lunch out of doors, and if this were done, the ladies would come and join the guns and a fairly sumptuous picnic lunch would be consumed. The King had made arrangements with the main house that two hot dishes should be sent down, and the rest of the meal would be cold, consisting of lobster salads or chicken mayonnaise for those who preferred it. If the weather was unpleasant, there were cottages throughout the estate with facilities for entertaining twenty or thirty sportsmen and their wives. King Edward even had an extension built on to the royal station at Wolferton to be used as a lunch-room whenever there was a big rabbit-shoot at the nearby Warren. Lunch at Windsor, when Queen Victoria's regime ended, was usually held in the Cranbourne Tower, and the food was sent from the royal kitchens.

After lunch, the ladies might be allowed to watch, though it does not sound to have been too much of a treat. As the pheasants flew in droves over the guns, the men were too busy to talk to wives and mistresses, who anyway had to stand in the right place or run the risk of being shot. Before smokeless powder was introduced they would be shrouded in acrid smoke, which at best smelt unpleasant, and which at worst could singe the eyebrows if an onlooker ventured too close. To round off the discomfort, the noise was appalling. To see someone hit by a falling pheasant was probably the nearest thing to fun, though, considering the quantities of birds being killed, even that did not happen very often. Nonetheless Lady Ailesbury took three months to recover when it happened to her, and the Dowager Lady Westmorland fared pretty poorly at Crichel. Yet, for all this, if we are to believe the *Liverpool Evening News*, the ladies were not always

Lunchtime at Bere Wood.

Lady Leconfield hating every minute.

Feeding the beaters, Rufford Abbey (Lord Savile's).

daunted. At Knowsley, when the guns were stationed some distance away, they 'evinced the keenest interest in the proceedings, and more than one of them mounted and followed on bicycle'. Generally speaking, though, they were expected to be passive spectators. Lady Fingall found herself beside the Prince of Wales (later King George V) at Elveden when he shot two partridges in front of him, turned, and shot two more behind. Overcome by such skill, she jumped up and slapped him on the back, 'and we shook hands and danced round for joy'. Sir Charles Cust, who had been watching, reproved her: 'Little lady, you must not do that. I have grown up on the steps of the throne and I can tell you that there are three kinds of people in the world. Blacks, whites, and royalties.'

Some women refused to play such a subservient role, and took up shooting themselves. In 1882 Queen Victoria wrote a disapproving letter to her daughter Princess Victoria, in which she said that it was acceptable for a lady to be a spectator, but only fast women shot. A similar sentiment was expressed by the seventy-year-old Lord Warwick in 1917: 'I have met ladies who shoot, and I have come to the conclusion, being no longer young and a staunch Conservative, that I would prefer them not to.' The Duchess of Bedford was a very keen shot, and she reported that 'it is impossible for a woman to do a long day's walking in comfort over the moors or in turnips in a skirt which is longer than eight inches below the knee'. Perhaps Queen Victoria was right after all.

The Merton gamebooks show that Mrs. William Garnier shot three partridges as early as 1845. Princess Radziwill shot regularly with Sir Frederick Milbank at Barningham. On 6 September 1889 she was the lowest scorer. She also shot less than anybody else on 13, 15 and 16

The ladies, Warter Priory, 1910.

Refreshment time at Lady
Curzon's: ginger beer for the
beaters, champagne for the guns.

August 1890. By 10 September 1891 she had improved – bottom equal with the vicar! One of the best, on the other hand, was Mrs. Willie Jameson, the wife of the millionaire yachtsman and a close friend of King Edward VII. Her speciality was driven partridges, and, whenever she was out, she took with her a little King Charles spaniel as retriever. It could manage partridges satisfactorily, but could only struggle with the size of a dead pheasant. Hares seem to have been altogether beyond it.

The impression which comes through is that women shot more regularly on the Continent than they did in England. Daisy of Pless seems always to have shot on her own estate at Fursenstein in Germany, and was constantly having new guns made for her by the best London gunmakers. Yet when she and her husband stayed at Chatsworth, he shot and she watched. Should anyone be ungallant enough to think that female was intrinsically less skilful at handling a gun, let Mrs. Hwfa Williams champion her sex: 'I was so successful at the *tir au sanglier* that the people at the Casino gave me a medal inscribed with the words "From the administration of Monte Carlo".

Irish aggression: Lady Mac-Calmont at Mount Juliet, 1910.

English phlegm: Lord
Ashburton and loaders.

You can imagine how proud I was.'

After the shooting came tea. The women appeared in their tea-
gowns. The plan was to see who could captivate the men with the
most stunning gown, and vast sums must have been spent. Mrs.
Williams reckoned them '*very* elaborate in design and pattern ... a
change after one's thick shooting clothes, and very becoming'. She
went on: 'We all took our best dresses when we went to Eaton, but try
as we would, it was useless to compete with Daisy. Her tea-gowns were
sans pareil; she knew exactly how to get the most striking effect from
the simplest things.' But even if Daisy Warwick won the battle in
the eyes of her own sex, the men were not always susceptible. Fatigue
drove most of them upstairs the moment they came home, and those
who remained for tea were usually more interested in reliving a shot-
by-shot account of their successes.

The physical penalties of the day's shooting should not be allowed
to pass without comment. It was perhaps not surprising that sportsmen who might discharge their guns 1,500 times in a single day were
subject to headaches. There is a sad story by Lord Rossmore which
happened in Ireland in the 1880s. 'Lord Iveagh (when he was Sir

The lady killers.

Edward Guinness) came to Rossmore and we were going to shoot four days in the week. On the first day my gamekeeper, Hughie Cusker, came up to me and said, pointing at Sir Edward, "Is he wrong in the head? – because he came up to me just now and said, 'Are you the head keeper and do you ever place the guns?' 'I do sometimes I says.' 'Well, whenever you're going to place me here's a sovereign for ye – put me where nothing can possibly come near me.' " . . . The reason for Sir Edward's strange request was that he had developed a splitting headache which made him feel so downright ill that his only desire was to be completely out of action.'

Interestingly, the very best shots of all did not suffer from headaches. After Lord Walsingham had shot 1,000 grouse in a day in 1888, he stayed up till 5 a.m. that night playing cards, and said that he had never felt better. Lord Ripon likewise never complained of headaches and put it down to the fact that he never drank before a big shoot (he must have been almost teetotal), and ate abstemiously. Perhaps this immunity should be treated with a certain reserve. After the record rabbit shoot at Blenheim the Duke of Marlborough wrote to H. S. Gladstone saying that none of the guns (the Duke himself, the young Duleep Singhs, Sir Robert Gresley and Stephen Wombwell) was tired or sore-shouldered. The Duchess of Marlborough, recalling the same incident from a disinterested standpoint, records that they all had splitting headaches. The Vicomte de Poucins de Lailly Loriet

92

Why women were not popular in the field.

wrote to *The Field* in 1908 with some more exotic ideas; a dose of antipyrine, and a piece of chewed up blotting paper placed between the upper lip and the front teeth was one suggestion. Sir Ralph Payne Gallwey mentions that Lord Leicester used to use the blotting paper trick to stop nose bleeds.

The preparations for the shooting houseparties were extensive, as even the largest houses seemed never quite big enough to hold everybody in comfort. Many of the older houses were, by today's standards,

somewhat primitive and it was usually more comfortable to stay in the home of some *nouveau riche*, who had seen that each guest had his own bathroom, than in the medieval splendour of a Warwick or Windsor Castle, where constipation was a positive blessing. One lady who was entertaining King Edward VII for the first time, and who had spent a fortune in refurnishing the entire house, ventured to ask him whether all was satisfactory. The King thought for a moment, and then said that it might be an idea to put a hook in the bathroom door,

Keith Hall, the Scottish seat of Lord Kintore.

so that he could hang up his dressing-gown. The lady was mortified.

One of the reasons the houseparties were so large was that each guest would bring a retinue of staff – sometimes as many as ten, including butler, liveryman, groom and personal maid. The servants lived their own lives within the walls of these houses, and protocol was observed quite as rigorously as it was with their masters. And so was precedence. Being a lady's maid to a plain untitled Miss meant you walked out last from hall. A friend of Lady Augusta Fane's overheard a valet call to the lady's maid in the next room, 'Hurry up, Ripon, you'll be late for supper; both the Abercorns are down.' It was the head butler who ruled these little kingdoms, retaining for himself only the most important jobs: choosing the wine with the host for dinner, carving the joint, terrifying the other servants. The butler at Henham was overheard instructing a young footman, 'Now, James, hold up your head and look as if you had ten thousand pounds a year and a deer park!' Ralph Bankes, by contrast, once had a less dignified butler at Kingston Lacey. At dinner there was a haunch of venison on the menu, and the host carved it himself. The butler, somewhat the worse for wear, lurched forward and seized the dish, saying thickly, 'You've as much idea of carvin' a haunch of venison as a rabbit 'as – let me 'ave a shot!' He attempted to stagger to the sideboard, dropped the dish and fell on top of it.

Sir Ralph Payne Gallwey had an unpalatable experience when he believed his butler was being dishonest. Sir Ralph had organised a fortnight's party in the north of Scotland, and towards the end of the first week the sherry decanter was only half full, although none of the guests was drinking any. It became clear that the butler was the culprit, and to ensure that it happened no more, the decanter was 'spiked' with an unmentionable liquid. To Sir Ralph's horror, the level in the decanter continued to fall. The butler was asked directly whether he had been taking the sherry. 'Yes', was the unexpected reply, 'and I have been putting two tablespoons in your soup every evening as your doctor ordered.'

While the servants jostled for position, the houseparty proper followed a predictable routine. It was not until the evening that the two sexes were reunited for any length of time. There was always something of an *entracte* between tea and the time to go and change for dinner. It was customary then to play cards; whist and bridge were particularly popular. Only the men played cards for serious money, and this invariably happened after dinner – it was possible to win or lose perhaps five shillings before dark; ruin at cards was reserved for later sessions.

The Cassano Orchestra was a regular feature at West Dean in Sussex. One evening, when George Cornwallis-West was coming down to dinner, he met the King on a landing, who said to him: 'What are you going to play tonight?' 'Bridge, I suppose, sir,' he answered. The

King looked round quickly and then burst out laughing and said, 'I took you for the man who conducts the band.'

Dinner was a formal affair, and jewels would be worn – this was universal, particularly after the Duchess of Marlborough who was wearing only a diamond crescent was asked by the Prince of Wales, 'The Princess has taken the trouble to wear a tiara. Why have you not done so?' The kitchens were invariably miles away from the dining room, and the problems which beset the hostess at Blenheim were typical of most of the country houses of the period. There it was a rule that dinner must not take longer than one hour. As the kitchen was at least three hundred yards from the dining room, and the meal consisted of eight courses, the difficulties were considerable. Two

Fancy dress dinner at a Crichel shooting party: Lord Alington as Captain Bluebeard.

97

Amateur dramatics: Sir John
Cotterell trying hard.

soups, one hot and one cold, were served simultaneously: these were
followed by two fish courses. After that, an entrée that was succeeded
by a meat dish. Usually the meat consisted of game in season, otherwise quails were imported from Egypt and ortolans from France. An
elaborate pudding followed, then a hot savoury which accompanied
the port. Dinner ended with peaches, plums, apricots, nectarines,
strawberries, raspberries, pears and grapes, all grouped in generous
pyramids among the flowers that adorned the table.

After dinner, the first evening was often the occasion for a ball;
but shooting and dancing are not good companions, and the ball
would be more for the benefit of the local county families than the
sportsmen, who made their excuses to retire early. The comparative
lack of opportunity for outside entertainment in these country houses
meant that new ways of passing the time were constantly in demand.
One of the more popular ideas was amateur dramatics. It is extraordinary how seriously these sophisticated people took these trifles,
which were usually written for the occasion. It was a form of entertainment much more enjoyed by the performers than the audience,
who had to see an indifferent play murdered by less than indifferent

acting; but it did at least have the advantage of keeping those who were not shooting busy at the rehearsals. Daisy Pless wrote in her diary, staying at Chatsworth, 'I have had no time to write, having had to rehearse hard every day. We acted last night after only three days rehearsing, while we ought to have had a week; it all went very well except in my monologue when I was alone on the stage for twenty minutes. I suddenly forgot my cue and the ass of a prompter who was not following lost the page and did not know where to find it, so I had to say, "Please give me the words"; some of them say that I stamped my foot and said "Damn the man!" but I am sure that I didn't.'

In the early 1890s the Royal Household staged *She Stoops to Conquer* and Queen Victoria graciously attended. Unfortunately she took exception to Captain Ponsonby's chucking Princess Louise under the chin. He received a message that he was not to indulge in such familiarity. The following morning, so concerned was he not to be thought a blackguard, he barely even cast his eyes in the Princess's direction. Another message followed, saying he was overdoing it the other way.

Both Princess Louise and Princess Beatrice were hopeless at learning their words. To overcome this, the other members of the cast learnt the Princesses' parts so that they could be helped out at critical moments. Unhappily, there was a point at which both were on stage together, and they both dried up. Anxious to cover up for them, the servants broke into long applause, and eventually the stage carpenter put an end to their misery by letting down the curtain.

Spending the night in these country houses was an experience in

An earl for 87 years: Lord Coventry and his wife on their Diamond Wedding.

itself. One evening at Elveden, Daisy Fingall was feeling rather ill following an oyster lunch with Lord Coventry. Very ill by the time she went to bed, she took stock of who was in the next-door rooms should she need help. Thinking that she could not disturb the Prince of Wales, and seeing a door marked 'the Marquis of Villalobar', she decided that in *extremis* she would seek help there. In the event she felt better and did not disturb him. The following morning she recounted to Sir Charles Cust how ill she had felt and how she had nearly wakened the Marquis. Instead of being sympathetic he stared at her and then roared with laughter and went across to tell the Prince of Wales the joke, which Lady Fingall did not altogether understand. It turned out that the Marquis, a remarkable man, had no legs, one hand, and no hair at all. The experience, had she called on him, would probably have killed her.

Lord Charles Beresford made one of the more embarrassing navigational blunders. Thinking to surprise one of his lady loves, he entered a darkened bedroom and sprang on to the bed shouting 'Cock-a-doodle-doo', only to be coolly received by its occupants, the Bishop of Chester and his wife. Although such behaviour was con-

A shooting party with Lady Violet Astor.

sidered indefensible in the royal homes, it was certainly practised elsewhere, and the methods used became more subtle as time went on. One lady arranged with her paramour that she would have a plate of sandwiches outside her door if the coast was clear for him to join her. By ill luck, a passing guest having no idea of their significance, ate them and continued on his way. Her lover, on seeing the empty plate, thought that this was intended as a dire warning, and accordingly returned to his room disappointed.

He was not the only one who was disappointed on such an occasion. Lord Rossmore remembered: 'Once I was invited to a country house where a lovely lady whom I greatly admired was also a guest. We were delighted to meet in this accidentally-done-for-the-purpose manner and arranged to have a tête-à-tête later to look at the stars. Well, I must have dropped off to sleep, because I was horrified to find it was 3 a.m., when I set out down the ghostly corridor to keep my appointment. I padded along and turned down the passage which led to the room where we planned to meet, but when I got there I noticed a man sitting on guard outside. He viewed me with a lowering brow, and then I grasped the fact that as he had not been asked to star gaze, he was determined to see who had. I pretended not to notice him, and walked on to the bathroom, where I took an early tub, and thought of many things I should like to have said to him.'

The sense of rendezvous could even add spice to innocence. Daisy Pless analyses it when she was sleeping in a different room from her husband at her parents' home at Newlands. 'There was something unusual in his having to come right along a passage, past other doors

101

BURBERRY

YARN-PROOFS ARE **IDEAL RAIN COATS** for Out-o'-Door Sport.

FREE-SHOT COAT

The Greatest Boon for **SHOOTING, GOLFING, FISHING,** and kindred exercises.

With PATENT PIVOT SLEEVE

Pronounced perfect by experts. Gets ahead of all other schemes for liberating arms and shoulders. Enables the wearer to move the arms with the greatest freedom.

"NIBLICK," "ILLUSTRATED SPORTING AND DRAMATIC NEWS." "I found, when swinging, a freedom under the arm which I have never before experienced in any other coat."

"H.G.H.," "GOLF ILLUSTRATED." "It must give a man a great advantage to play in such a coat as this."

"THE BADMINTON MAGAZINE." "The trial rendered it simply ridiculous to think of shooting, fishing, or playing golf in any other garment."

Gives the most ABUNDANT and SATISFYING freedom of arm in WHATEVER POSITION, and a feeling of LIBERTY and DETACHMENT hitherto UNAPPROACHED. Even overhead reaching does not bring any strain on the body of the coat.

PRINCE HAT.

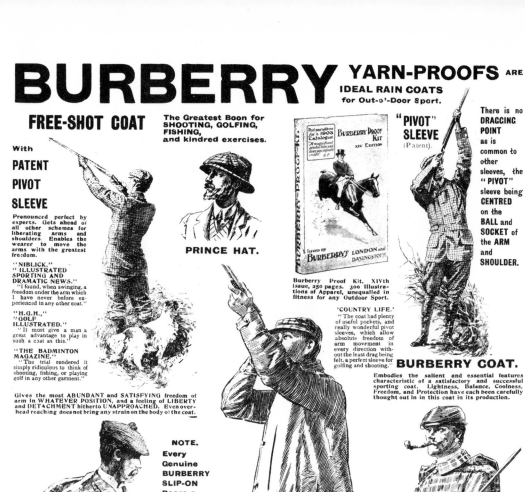

Burberry Proof Kit, XIVth issue, 250 pages. 300 Illustrations of Apparel, unequalled in fitness for any Outdoor Sport.

'COUNTRY LIFE.' "The coat had plenty of useful pockets, and really wonderful pivot sleeves, which allow absolute freedom of arm movement in every direction without the least drag being felt, a perfect sleeve for golfing and shooting."

"PIVOT" SLEEVE (Patent).

There is no DRAGGING POINT as is common to other sleeves, the "PIVOT" sleeve being CENTRED on the BALL and SOCKET of the ARM and SHOULDER.

BURBERRY COAT.

Embodies the salient and essential features characteristic of a satisfactory and successful sporting coat. Lightness, Balance, Coolness, Freedom, and Protection have each been carefully thought out in in this coat in its production.

NOTE. Every Genuine BURBERRY SLIP-ON Bears a Burberry Label.

BURBERRY HIGHLANDER.

With Straps to cross over chest to allow Cape to be thrown back (for shooting). Invaluable either for keeping out rain or adding warmth.

BURBERRY SLIP-ON.

After years of world-wide trial in storm and flood, the Slip-on holds the field the Sportsman's best all-round over-garment extant. Ample in cut, it shields the wearer completely from collar to gaiters.

Extremely light, the wearer is quite unhampered, absolute freedom being given for quick movement. Its resistance to rain is unequalled by anything short of oilskins.

BURBERRY CAPE.

Fitted with a double front, or inner waistcoat, to protect front of body when the wings are thrown back and allow freedom of arm for shooting. Large openings admit of easy access to under pockets, and control of the wings is retained in wind by buttoning them round the wrists, forming them into sleeves.

31, HAYMARKET, LONDON: and BASINGSTOKE.

Advertisement in *Country Life.*

The Duke of Rutland in his butt.

and then leave quietly on tip toe as if he (and I too) had been doing something wrong; there is a little air of mystery about it which is amusing, and therefore more tempting.'

Dress was another area where the proprieties were important. King Edward VII was brought up to believe that slipshod dressing was the mark of bad breeding. His subjects came to defer to his personal tastes, which is why we leave the bottom button of our waistcoats undone, and press our trousers down the middle rather than the side. The significance of his lead in these matters can be seen from the fuss which erupted over Quiller Orchardson's portrait entitled *Four Generations*. It was rumoured, before the picture was generally shown, that the heir apparent was wearing a frock coat and brown boots. Peace was only restored when assurances were given that the Prince's boots had in fact been painted black, and that he only wore brown boots in the country. Apart from one rare lapse at Marienbad in 1903, of which the *Tailor and Cutter* wrote 'Loyal subjects must sincerely hope that His Majesty has not brought this outfit home', the King's ideas set the tone for the society in which he moved.

103

Robert Willan and the Duke of York (King George VI) at Balmoral, 1915.

The Duke of York shooting at Wilton House, 1926.

It was the ladies, predictably, who had the keenest responsibilities. A shooting party entailed a breakfast suit, usually an elegant costume in velvet or silk, then tweeds for lunch with the guns and for two cold drives in the afternoon. These would be followed by the extravagant tea-gowns, then finally a satin or brocade full length evening dress. Since it was considered bad form to wear the same gown more than once, and most shooting parties lasted for four days, it meant an outlay of sixteen dresses for a single house party.

By the 1890s, the men's shooting dress had become standardised. Tailcoats and waistcoats, once the outfit of every shooting man, were still to be seen on many of the estate's keepers but the more useful Harris Tweed shooting suits had replaced them among the guns. Each shooting man would have these made by his own tailor, to his own specifications, and so there was still plenty of variety to be seen on a shooting field. The royal family, and particularly the Prince of Wales (King George V) wore shooting spats, and these were quickly taken up by others, including Lord de Grey and the Duleep Singhs.

Only a certain latitude was allowed on the shooting field, however, and eccentricity was frowned upon. Lord Rossmore fancied a pair of jodhpurs which were popularised by the Duke of Connaught when he came back from India. Rossmore had some made in black buckskin,

Varieties of tweed on the shooting field.

and he was so pleased with the way they looked that he wore them out shooting at Elveden. When King Edward VII spied them, he came over and said, 'I'm glad to see, Rossmore, that you are using up your old evening trousers to make shooting leggings.' His hat, too, came in for a similar badinage. General Strachey, who was also shooting at Elveden said of it 'By jove! I am not a wealthy man, but I would willingly give £1,000 to have the impertinent audacity to wear that hat.' Lord Suffield was also renowned for the eccentricity of his hats. One, which he wore at Sandringham, was described as 'incredibly awful, looking as if it had been fashioned by a pickaxe and shovel and rolled over by a dozen or more buses'.

The code of Edwardian society may seem, to present day thinking, preposterous. But Edwardian society had the confidence to be preposterous. Solecisms mattered, because although participation may not always have been pleasurable, exclusion was invariably painful.

Count Canisy dressed to kill.

The influence of Savile Row spread far: the Czar wearing a shooting jacket especially designed for him in London.

Lord Houghton once wrote:

> On the first of September one Sunday morn
> I shot a pheasant in standing corn
> Without a licence. Contrive who can
> Such a cluster of crimes against God and Man

Had the villain missed the pheasant the reaction could have been worse. The Edwardians liked success. The formula for such success was once quaintly described as 'get on, get honour, get honest'. And on the shooting field the same was true. If you could hit them all in the head, you were mentioned in every society memoir published between 1890 and 1930. It was the Duke of Portland's head keeper who when asked why the bags were very small in the Duke's absence, replied, 'Some of the officers didn't kill as much as they could eat.' Lord Loreburn was so upset when his guests started to miss that he tried to cancel the shoot in mid-drive because he refused to show the birds to guests who were not worthy of them. It was only with the greatest difficulty that the head keeper persuaded him to let the shoot continue.

It was not a good idea, either, to cause a dead bird to fall in an undesired direction. The most undesirable direction of all was anywhere near King Edward VII. Even Lord Ripon could be guilty of this. When His Majesty was out shooting in a bath chair, having suffered an injury to his foot while shooting at Windsor, Lord Ripon killed an exceptionally high pheasant which seemed about to fall on his head. Mercifully it fell a few inches wide but hit the arm of the bath chair, burst open and covered the King with blood and feathers. For a moment it seemed the King might burst open as well.

106

The present Lord Albemarle recalls that he was invited as a young man to shoot at West Dean Park, the Sussex home of Mr. Willie James. At the first drive 'before I could reflect, a very high bird skimmed above my head from the left, and fell dead at King Edward's feet. The worst catastrophe of my life! The drive over! What could I do? Feeling and looking like a condemned criminal, I approached the Presence to find the kindest smile and forbearance indicating that such events must sometimes happen.' (Incidentally, Lord Albemarle clearly took this to heart; the author's father, as a young boy, did the same thing to him, only in this case it was a hen pheasant on a 'cocks only' day. The kindness and understanding were repeated.)

King Edward VII had a technique for guests who shot hen pheasants on 'cocks only' days, a regulation decreed for the last days' shooting at Sandringham. At the beginning of the century, one of the party on such an occasion was Sir Somerville Gurney of North Runcton Hall, who was unable to resist one of the highest hens that came over him. He shot it, and this was observed by King Edward. At the end of the drive, the King winked at him and said quietly 'Ah Gurney, you always were a great man for the ladies!'

On the whole it was better not to shoot any of the assembly. This was a lesson which was generally instilled from an early age: the children were taught gun craft by their local gamekeeper who was

West Dean Park: Lord Dudley showing Master Edward James how to shoot; Mrs. Willie James watches.

Miss Queenie Robinson shooting her father, Old Buckenham Hall, Norfolk.

well able to instruct them in the principles of safety. Sir Shane Leslie was brought up to this in Ireland, and remembered for the rest of his life the horror when his gun went off accidentally and nearly shot the eccentric classical don Professor Mahaffy. Mahaffy did not seem in the least put out and his only comment was 'Two inches lower and you'd have blown half the Greek out of Ireland.'

The closing ritual of the houseparty usually involved the Visitors' Book. This seemingly insignificant thing was an object of terror because, in addition to their names, each visitor had to express some sentiment in writing, and to state the object of the visit. Those who were unused to it dreaded the performance: a certain Miss Vernon wrote in desperation in the Duke of Cleveland's book at Raby

'Who'll burn the book?'
'I,' said Di Vernon,
'If the duchess won't look;
I'll burn the book.'

A page from Lord Kintore's visitors' book, Keith Hall. No witty comments but all the right people.

Not everybody was as witty as the gentleman who stayed in a large, rather draughty house, reminiscent of St. Pancras station, and who wrote 'C'est magnifique, mais ce n'est pas la gare.' Fritz Ponsonby thought that the writing of *bons mots* was nothing more than a trick, and that most people who stayed at country houses regularly always had something ready. The King he described as an old hand at this game. So, too, was Lord Rosebery, who was staying with the Duke of Cleveland (the Duchess of Cleveland was his mother) when he wrote under the heading 'Object of the Visit' the following:

> To see their Graces
> And to shoot their Grouses.

It was good of him to put it that way round.

The gamekeeper in 1845; tough, independent and not above the temptation of cock-fighting.

7
The Supporting Cast

The gamekeeper has been a part of the English countryside for a long time. An Act of Parliament of 1683 allowed gentleman above the rank of esquire to appoint gamekeepers 'who shall have power within the manor to seize guns nets and engines kept by unqualified persons to destroy game, and, by a warrant of the Justice of the Peace, to search in the daytime houses of unqualified persons upon the ground of suspicion'. By the beginning of the eighteenth century it became clear that landowners were using the statute to employ private armies of bodyguards, under the guise of gamekeepers. Parliament therefore intervened again, and per estate allowed only one keeper, who was permitted for the first time to kill game as well as protect it.

The early gamekeeper was an expensive luxury; his master had to pay a licence fee of one guinea annually for having him, with a further fee of three guineas if he was empowered to kill game. In addition, His Majesty's Government was entitled to 6/- for each pedigree dog that was kept, and 4/- for the rest. By an Act of 1798, a penalty of £50 was payable by any wilful omission from 'the List of Dogs'. A fine was similarly incurred if the landowner miscounted his staff – though here the penalty was only £30. English gentleman were expected to keep a closer eye on their dogs than their servants.

In the early days, there was little science about the job, and one of the gamekeeper's springtime duties was to walk round and collect the pheasant eggs from the wild birds' nests on the estate. There was always a temptation to go across the boundary on to neighbouring territory, and this was the cause of many disputes. The 5th Lord Walsingham on one occasion held a semi-judicial enquiry in his business room. The room was filled with keepers from both estates, and formal evidence was given by both sides. At the end a verdict was given and since Lord Walsingham was both judge and plaintiff, it is perhaps not surprising that the judgment was in his favour.

There is one early record of a woman gamekeeper. In the 1820s the Holkham estate had one, Polly Fishbourne, an imposing woman

The lady gamekeeper.

whose flashing eyes and close-cropped hair intimidated the North Norfolk countryside, including it seems, the cattle. She once saved a man from a bull which was goring him. She approached it, and, as it saw her, it cowered away. The animal had apparently once attempted to charge her, but she lodged a charge of small shot in its muzzle! Her aggression was generally directed against the local poachers whom, no doubt, she treated with equal consideration. On one occasion, at least, we see a subtler approach. A Norfolk game-preserver offered Polly a shilling piece for one hundred pheasants' eggs. She took the money, and gave the man one hundred guinea-fowl eggs instead. An honest girl, she gave the shilling to the squire of Holkham (in those days plain Mr. Coke).

With the advent of driven shooting, the need for gamekeepers increased, and their numbers grew considerably. They were recruited from a variety of trades, with a surprising number drawn from the casual labour force employed in building the railways – for this was the age of the railway expansion. From this background young Edward Raine became head keeper on Sir George Musgrave's Edenhall estate which was already famous for the size of its bags in the 1860s. The same was true on the Duke of Portland's Caithness estate at

King of the Castle: the head keeper at Warter Priory, with fruits of victory.

Langwell. The head keeper there, Donald Ross, was acquired by Portland's predecessor in the early 1850s, and under him the estate was effectively managed for the first time. The shooting there consisted almost entirely of grouse, and Ross set about the systematic destruction of the vermin of the moors, particularly of the crows and foxes which wrought so much havoc among young birds. In 1859 he also introduced for the first time the technique of heather burning long before it was generally realised that the burning of the heather resulted in a plentiful supply of young heather essential to the preservation of grouse stock. The results were not long in showing. In the 1840s, two guns walking over dogs could expect to come home with between ten and twenty brace of grouse. By 1871, the annual total of grouse was 2,230, and that figure continued to rise throughout the remainder of the century.

These head keepers in Scotland were given a great deal of authority. Not only were they in charge of the grouse shooting, but were usually also responsible for the fishing, and, most important of all, the stalking. Many of them had personalities to match. Donald Ross, the Langwell keeper, did not like Lord Cole very much, and so took malicious pleasure in writing to him as 'Dear Lord Coal'. On one occasion Ross took exception to the French chef which the Duke of Portland had brought with him to Scotland. A commotion in the kitchen revealed Ross sitting on top of the terrified chef, banging his head against the floor, and bellowing 'Remember Waterloo!' Lady Bolsover, who was staying in the Duke's houseparty, was horrified

113

Counting the bag at Stonor Park.

and asked Portland to get rid of the objectionable keeper. The Duke knew better, and it was the cook who was ticked off for upsetting Ross.

A man of similar temperament was the head ghilly at Balmoral. The original keeper was John Grant, who controlled all the sport at Balmoral and Invercauld, which the Royal Family rented from the Duke of Fife. He was succeeded by his son Arthur, who was dedicated to his job and not a man to suffer fools gladly. When King Edward VII's younger brother, the Duke of Connaught, was staying at Balmoral in 1915, Grant accompanied him stalking. The Royal Duke missed two easy stags. It was not the moment of greatest glory in a career not sweetened with success, and Mr. Grant summarised it pungently: 'Ye blitherin' idiot, you've ruined the whole thing.' Sir Derek Keppel was likewise castigated for showing too much behind when crawling towards the quarry. The reason, Sir Derek later explained, was that he had just acquired a new shooting suit and was anxious not to acquaint it too closely with the undulations of Deeside. The author's grandfather, Mr. Willan, who spent some time at Balmoral noted gloomily in his diary, 'Grouse tomorrow. I hope that it is not a case of "What, Willan? No birrrds at all?"'

The English keepers do not seem to have been quite so terrifying. But pottering round their masters' estates, which fairly described their activities in the first part of the century, played no part of the lives of the keepers of the big *battue* of fifty years later. We have a detailed record of the keeper's task in looking after the pheasants on Lord Rothschild's estate at Tring. Lord Rothschild had been a friend of the young Duleep Singhs in their undergraduate days at Cambridge in the late 1880s. They had both learnt their love of shooting on the latter's estate at Elveden, at that time still held in trust for the Prince, and Rothschild had to pay £10 a day for the privilege of shooting on the land. When he inherited Tring, Lord Rothschild's chief interest was pheasants. It was he who had discovered the type of pheasant known as the Mellanistic Mutant, which he came across, dead, in the Cambridge market. He had the birds stuffed and mounted in the hall at Tring where they aroused much comment. Although there are other reports of Mellanistics in the 1880s, they do not seem to have been seen again until the early 1920s, since which time they have become quite common.

At Tring, the head gamekeeper was also *ex officio* the head woodman, so that the interests of the sport and timber did not conflict. The underkeepers were solely engaged in game preservation. One of the most important aspects of the breeding of the pheasants was the type of food the birds should be given. At Tring the pheasant chicks were fed first on boiled egg and biscuit, and later on the best grain. This was a luxury which had to be suspended when England was being slowly starved by the German submarine campaign during the latter part of the First World War. Regulation 2f of the Defence of

116

the Realm Act forbade the feeding of game birds with grain. It continued, of course, in some places and there were prosecutions. In April 1917 Lord Pirrie's pheasants at Whitley Park were discovered to be feeding off grain. The head keeper, James MaClean, was fined £10, as was the corn dealer who supplied the grain, and even the labourer who fed the birds was fined £1. Lord Pirrie said he had no idea such wickedness was going on, and was acquitted.

As in so many other places, the land at Tring was not naturally able to support a great weight of wild pheasants, and so there was a great emphasis on the rearing of birds. The laying pheasants would be penned before the start of the season on 1 October. About 275 birds, each expected to lay about thirty good eggs, would be so treated, being put into an area of about two and a half acres where they would

Keepers at Quidenham, 1911.

117

A covey of keepers, 1901.

remain until 1 March. Their wings were clipped to ensure that they did not fly away, and their pen surrounded by netting of a height of at least seven feet. In March the birds would be moved to much smaller pens, each containing about twenty hen birds and five cock pheasants. When the eggs first appeared, it was the job of the underkeepers to go round each morning and collect them and put them in batches of fourteen under a broody farmyard hen. When they hatched they would be transferred to another pen, where they were nursed to maturity. Three keepers were put in charge of each batch of 2,000 birds; two to tend the young birds by day, the other to keep a constant vigil throughout the night to guard against vermin or poachers. The job of the keeper had come a long way from 1818 when Scott could accuse the race of keepers as being 'the most considerable poachers in the country'. By 1880 these men were professionals; at Holkham each keeper was responsible for 1,150 eggs, and was expected to produce 1,000 pheasants for the guns at the end of

118

the day. There was not much margin for error.

The success of these keepers was particularly impressive in parts of the country not at all conducive to wild pheasants. At the Gladstone estate of Fasque in Kincardineshire, eight guns killed over 3,000 pheasants on 18 November 1911. Little wonder that keepers were accused of being a breed of butchers, wanting the guns placed so that there could be no chance of missing. It was the host who was more concerned that the birds flew as sportingly as possible, but, if the guns could not shoot straight, more often than not it was the keeper who got the blame for a poor bag at the end of the day

At some places it was the practice of the host to allow his head keeper to place the guns, and this position of responsibility was often abused because it meant that the guests who the keeper thought would tip him heaviest at the end of the day got the best places. George Cornwallis-West, who was extremely well connected but had no title himself, was particularly averse to the system. It meant that he was sent with the beaters every drive. He did however, pull off one practical joke at the keeper's expense. He had been given a Browning self-loading gun from which it was possible to fire five consecutive shots as quickly as one could pull the trigger. A plot was laid on for the benefit of the keepers. It was settled that Cornwallis-West's neighbour would say at the beginning of the day, 'What a fool you are to come out shooting grouse with a single-barrel gun!' 'I was to say nothing but, at the first point, was to loose off all five barrels as quickly as I could, while he was not to fire at all. We were anxious to see the effect of this performance on the Scottish keepers, who had never even heard of a self-loading gun, let alone seen one. All went beautifully. At the very first point an old cock grouse got up, and I fired off five barrels in about four seconds. The man who was working the dogs fell back in the heather in pure surprise; the other ghillies

Wildfowling.

sat down. The head keeper's remark was, "Eh gosh! what a terrible weepon!" '

The science with which the keepers carried out their job was nowhere better seen than at Sandringham, which had the added advantage of a landlord who was personally interested in the build-up and organisation of the shoots. The head keeper, Mr. Jackson, was appointed in 1871, and remained head keeper at Sandringham right up to the First World War. He was given a house on the estate; in fact he did rather better than the keeper of the kennels, Mr. Brunsdon, who was housed in what had been the monkey house. At a more modest level, each farm had its own keeper with one or two assistants. A cottage was built for each of them. As well as the usual tasks of rearing the birds and vermin control, they reported to Jackson the weight of game sighted on their farm, and Jackson in turn reported this back to the King. On the basis of this information, it could be decided what was the best way of driving the estate.

At Sandringham, on the day before a big shoot, an order would be passed through the whole estate forbidding all work on the land for fear of disturbing the game. On the day of the shoot itself, a virtual curfew would be placed on the estate, and nobody, except the beaters, would be allowed to show himself on the roads and no machinery was allowed to run. The drives themselves were like miniature battles. Jackson, in the style of the traditional general, would appear mounted, riding backwards and forwards on a brown cob to organise the line of beaters. The flankers had red or blue flags to indicate which

Cartridge boys replenishing their master's supply, Crichel.

flank they were covering. The keepers were dressed in the Royal livery
of green and gold. The beaters wore smocks, and each wore a hatband
of red so that a stray peasant wandering by could not illicitly join in
the fun without being discovered.

Gentleman who went to big shoots took at least three guns with
them, and sometimes four, and this entailed a fair amount of organisation. On these big days, the 'guns' would have two (or three) loaders,
and a boy to hold the bag of cartridges open at the end of the line. On
smaller days, only one loader would be necessary.

These men would most usually be drawn from the household,
being footmen or gardeners when not engaged in sporting activities. They were often treated pretty roughly. It is a fact that the
most experienced loader cannot load as quickly as his master can
shoot, and a gentleman does not like watching pheasants stream over
his head while being forced to watch with an empty gun. Sometimes,
when the cartridge stuck in the breech of a gun, the loader who had
not brought a cartridge extractor with him could be in serious difficulties. Even getting a cartridge wrong end up was easy enough while
trying to load a gun under pressure, with birds and bangs and curses
everywhere. This was the advice of an old hand to loaders: 'Should

Beaters artistically and usefully clad.

your gentleman get impatient and call out, take no notice, but calmly go on loading. After the stand, tell your gentleman that you were sorry to keep him waiting, and explain the reason. A good sportsman is always a gentleman, and he knows what it means to get a cartridge wrong end up. On subsequent occasions, he might not worry his loader when he was placed in a similar predicament.' The article ends with what must be the supreme example of wishful thinking: 'The loader may rest assured that, though his gentleman may not say much in words, his efforts are always appreciated.'

Not everybody used retainers to load for them. Lord Dudley's collection included the famous St. Andrews golfer, Andrew Kirkcaldy, and – even more oddly – Carl Jakse, his Austrian haircutter. Jakse proved to be a mistake, for when the haircutter was loading for him during a partridge drive, Eddy Dudley fired at a partridge which was too close, and blew it to pieces. As it fell at his feet, he kicked it into a ditch, hoping that the Duke of Portland who was his neighbour would not notice. At the end of the drive the Duke, who had shot six birds, asked Eddy what his luck had been, and was told that he had killed six birds too. 'Just then we heard the hairdresser calling out "Milor! milor!" He was holding fragments of a bird by its one remaining leg, and explained "See, milor! I have found another piece in the ditch. So I think milor now has one bird more than His Grace." I am afraid Eddy did not hear the last of this for a very long time!'

Gentlemen's behaviour to their servants had improved since the time of William III (died 1704), who would strike his attendants with a cane if something angered him. On one occasion William III was out shooting with a somewhat mealy-mouthed French attendant, whose job was to look after the guns and the dogs, and load for His Majesty. In those days the fowling-piece had to be fed with powder and shot, but this time the unfortunate Frenchman omitted to bring any shot. He loaded away, and every time a partridge flew away, the gun made a satisfactory bang, and there was the usual puff of smoke; not surprisingly, however, none of the birds fell. The attendant, who had failed to connect the absence of shot with the King's failure, exclaimed with ever-increasing wonder, 'I did never, no never did I see

Beaters having lunch on Lord Craven's estate.

His Majesty miss before.' His fate is not recorded.

The gun and the loaders would usually work as a team, and when the two had been together for some length of time, something of a team spirit would grow between them. One gun who had missed a great many birds by the end of a day's shooting said to his loader: 'Dear me, I'm afraid I haven't shot at all well today.' 'No,' said his loader, 'if we go on like that, we'd better give it up!' The loader was right. The success of a shot could depend quite a lot on the skill of the loader in being able to keep the front man 'fed' with a loaded gun. King Edward VII had a favourite loader for years, a dour Scot

called Peter Robinson, and when he was loading, the King shot noticeably better. After he retired, he was replaced by a man called, ironically, Mr. Prince. When King George v shot at Sandringham he employed one of the estate's agricultural workers as his loader. This man happened to be almost identical in appearance to King George. At any rate, the loader grew his beard in the same style as the King, and, whenever they appeared together, they always wore exactly the same clothing. It amused the King to see his guests unsure of whether they were talking to their monarch or an estate worker.

The loader was required to do more than place cartridges in a gun,

Feeding the beaters, Warter Priory.

and pass it to its owner. Mr. Singer wrote: 'When out loading he must be keen, ever on the alert, and when at a stand waiting for birds to come over he should, figuratively speaking, be his master's second eyes. All his faculties should be concentrated on the drive. Being slightly behind his master, he can often see birds first, and by calling "Left", "Right", or "Over", can enable him to get a shot he might otherwise lose. Being behind he will also know in which direction his master will shoot, and, if in the way, should duck his head. In partridge driving it is often necessary to do this, as birds come low and sharp over a hedge. He has to get into all sorts of positions, quite the reverse of comfortable. At one time he is crouching on the ground behind his master, at another in a ditch in front or under a low hedge.'

The ideal was not always reached. At one drive on the Cawdor Moors near Nairn, on a very windy day, with the birds coming with the wind, Lord Warwick shot a high bird right in front of him and, without waiting to see the result of the shot, turned half round and aimed at another, which he missed. 'Almost as I pressed the trigger,' he wrote, 'I received a tremendous blow on the side of my face that fairly knocked me over in the butt. My loader pulled me to to my feet, and I realised that the bird I had shot at first, falling dead through the air while travelling at the rate of an express train, had struck me as it fell. Very dazed, and a little angry I said to my loader: "Didn't you see that bird coming?" "Yes m'lord," was the unexpected reply, "I did see it coming, so I hid behind your lordship." '

The most important aspect of the loader's skill concerned safety. It was certainly not unknown for loaders to shoot their masters while loading overquickly, and it was even commoner for neighbouring guns or attendants to receive the contents of an accidental discharge. It was thus important that the loader never allowed the guns to point in the direction of anyone. It was also considered essential (indeed, it still is) that the gun should pass both to and from the shooter in a 'safe state'. It was said of Lord Ripon, no doubt by those envious of his skill, that the guns were passed to him cocked and ready for firing. If that is true, and it probably was, it might be seen as the prerogative of a man who prepared to get up at dawn and practice the best way of doing it!

It is hard to realise how many people were involved in these big shoots. The majority were beaters. Most of these would be farm labourers who worked on the landowner's estate, and for them it was a welcome change from the drudgery of farm husbandry – particularly if it was known that the team of guns was safe. Beaters were very vulnerable to reckless guns, and they tended to treat any wounds philosophically. 'Lor, master's got me again!' was heard on one grouse moor at the turn of the century. Others did not seem to realise the danger they were in. One old boy, complimenting his employer's

The game cart, Studley Royal, Yorkshire.

shooting, said, ''E do shoot wonderful close, sir, why, he knocked the stick out of my 'and and never touched me!'

It often happened that there were not sufficient men on the estate to provide enough beaters, flankers, markers and so forth, and some had to be brought in from outside. When old Lady Ailesbury was out at Sandringham in the 1890s, she commented that the beaters, in their blue twill smocks, reminded her of Frenchman. The Prince of Wales smiled and said. 'How clever of you, Lady A! that's just what they are. We can't get sufficient beaters here so we have to import some from France every year.'

The beaters were a vital part of the organisation of the day, and it was clear, too, that they had minds of their own. It was not unknown for them to go on strike for more pay: this happened at Cahir in Scotland (for sixpence per man per day) and, on this occasion at least, they got it. On one estate it was usual to dress the beaters in white smocks, each man with a large letter printed on his clothing – A, B, C, D, etc. – so they would be easier to manoeuvre in the middle of a hectic drive. The beaters resented this, feeling that it made them look like convicts, but the practice went on. One day, when the team of guns emerged with the ladies from lunch, they found the beaters so grouped that the guests were left in no doubt as to what the beaters thought of them.

Lord Rossmore had a bad experience with his beaters in Ireland. He had a poisonous Scottish keeper who 'turned out a regular gas bag and a deuced lazy fellow into the bargain'. The beaters were anxious to be rid of him and so they waited until the big grouse drive of a day when Rossmore was entertaining the Duke of Connaught. 'The guns went to their places, but were astonished to see crowds of birds passing over butts a quarter of a mile away. Then the line of drivers came in view, and we saw that they were really driving to the wrong butts. All the men were profuse in their apologies for making such a mistake, but as each man had driven the same ground for years, it was somewhat inexplicable, and it was not until the next season that I learnt that they had intentionally taken advantage of the keeper's ignorance so that I should get rid of him. Their plan was successful.'

Lord Massereene and Ferrard was in the habit of numbering rather than lettering his beaters on his estate at Castle Antrim. His excellence at shooting was marred, particularly in later years, by an affection for alcohol. Unfortunately this weakness was often highlighted in

One of the pioneers of the use of motor cars for shooting was John, Lord Montagu of Beaulieu, seen here sitting in his 1901 Daimler. Others in the shooting party include Mr. Thomas Thorpe, Sir Thomas Troubridge Bt., Mr. Heathley Noble and Mr. Reginald Hargraves.

but it was not so easy on hilly terrain.

a ritual which Lord Massereene would perform at the shoot. All the beaters would be marshalled to their employer who sat with a row of bottles and glasses in front of him.

'Well No. 1, what's yours?' Massereene would enquire.

'Anything your lordship pleases.'

'Well No. 1, judging from the look of you, brandy's yours,' and he reached for the bottle, poured out some into a glass and drank it, saying 'Yes, that's brandy.' He then refilled the glass and handed it to the beater. The same thing went on with the others, except that the drinks were varied, and Massereene would insist upon sampling them all first, with most unbalancing results.

One of the reasons for dressing the beaters up in medieval, or distinctive garb was to stop unauthorised individuals from joining in the fun, which could be disastrous on a shoot which required concerted movements to ensure success. The head keeper might be able to exclude uninvited beaters but it was never possible to exclude the public from taking part in the shoots. In an age which was particularly conscious of its social superiors, the whole countryside would come to watch a big houseparty out shooting, and in this respect miners seem to have been particularly inquisitive. Both at Welbeck and Himley they were a regular feature of the shooting. That gentleman adventurer, Moreton Frewen, wrote of Himley. 'I found myself playing up to an alarmingly critical gallery. The coverts on one side are hemmed in by coal pits, and scores, perhaps even hundreds of miners collected behind the guns, betting on the shots, full of vociferous approval if the performance was good.' The strain of a

The old ways: walking up partridges and hares, September 1909.

public gallery proved too much for Frewen's neighbour and the head keeper quickly replaced him with a more experienced shot. 'Happily, both he and I shot our best and the crowd was in a few moments sympathetic and approving.'

When King Edward VII was shooting with Lord Stamford at Bradgate, the master of the works at Leicester gave his men a half holiday, and they came out literally in their thousands to see the sport. One fifty-acre field was crammed with spectators and the afternoon shooting completely ruined. Lord Stamford asked Lord de Grey and another gun if they minded going into the crowd and guarding that side of the covert. As they shot the pheasants going over them, the birds flew among the crowd, who snatched at them and tore them to pieces in their eagerness to get hold of them. It was somewhat foggy, and several people climbed up into the trees to obtain a better view.

De Grey's neighbour, not noticing this, were extremely surprised when, firing what he never doubted to be a perfectly safe shot well up in the air, he heard a voice from above crying out, 'Hi! hi! That was too near!'

But there were direct hits. When King Edward VII was shooting with Sir Ernest Cassel at Six Mile Bottom, he shot a beater. The King had been having an animated conversation with a lady friend, who suddenly, and unwisely, pointed out a hare. The King, not realising that the beaters were so close, shot at it. There was a yell, and an aged beater, who evidently knew perfectly well who had shot him, came out of the spinney holding his knee. His Majesty, not realising what had happened, had turned aside, and resumed his conversation. Sir George Holford, one of the King's equerries, went up to him and said 'Do you know, sir, you've shot a beater?' The beater (it was subsequently discovered he was very little hurt) doubtless saw prospects of a life annuity and continued to moan. The King was much upset, and the man was removed and received adequate compensation. There is a great skill in being in the right place at the right time.

The end of the day – Lord Carnarvon's estate at Highclere.

Appendix 1
Records

The big shoots were a curious phenomenon which dominated the winter months of English Society for about forty years. It passed, however, and left little in its train. Those who had partaken, and who looked back in old age from another generation, felt guilty about it. Lord Warwick wrote, 'My early years were given to amusement. I suppose it sounds shocking nowadays.' The Duke of Portland went further and said, 'When I look back at the game book, I am quite ashamed of the enormous number of pheasants we some times killed. This is a form of shooting which I have no desire to repeat.'

It was said of the shooting world at the time, 'Up gets a guinea, bang goes a penny halfpenny, and down comes half-a-crown.' Thus, on a day when 4,000 pheasants were shot, we may presume that the butchers of Leadenhall Market gave 4,000 half-crowns for what had once been 4,000 guineas. What happened to the difference? It went in entertaining the guests, and posterity has been left with nothing except these extraordinary statistics.

PHEASANTS			
PLACE	DATE	HOME OF	TOTAL
Hall Barn (Bucks)	18 Dec. 1913	Lord Burnham	3,937
Warter Priory (Yorks)	5 Dec. 1909	Lord Nunburnholme	3,824
Sandringham (Norfolk)	4 Nov. 1896	Prince of Wales	3,114
Tot Magyar (Hungary)	10 Dec. 1909	Count Karolyi	6,125

PARTRIDGES			
Holkham (Norfolk)	7 Dec. 1905	Lord Leicester	1,671
Welbeck (Notts)	10 Oct. 1906	Duke of Portland	1,504
The Grange, Alresford (Hants)	4 Nov. 1897	Lord Ashburton	1,461
Sandringham (Norfolk)	10 Nov. 1905	Prince of Wales	1,342
St. Johann (Hungary)	1892?	Baron Hirsch	2,870

RED GROUSE			
Littledale (Lancs)	12 Aug. 1915	Lord Sefton	2,929
Broomhead (Yorks)	27 Aug. 1913	R. H. Rimington-Wilson	2,843
Broomhead (Yorks)	24 Aug. 1904	R. H. Rimington-Wilson	2,748
Roan Fell (Scotland)	30 Aug. 1911	Duke of Buccleuch	2,523

RABBITS			
Blenheim (Oxon)	7 Oct. 1898	Duke of Marlborough	6,943
Rhiwlas (Wales)	1885	Mr. Lloyd Price	5,086

HARES			
Holkham (Norfolk)	19 Dec. 1877	Lord Leicester	1,215

SHOOTING ALONE			
PLACE	DATE	PERSON	TOTAL
Elveden (Suffolk)	8 Sept. 1876	Maharajah Duleep Singh	780 Partridges
Bluberhouses (Yorks)	30 Aug. 1888	Lord Walsingham	1,070 Grouse
Wemmergill (Yorks)	20 Aug. 1872	Sir Fred. Milbank	190 Grouse (1 Drive)
St Johann (Hungary)	1893	Lord de Grey	240 Partridges (1 Drive)
Grandtully (Scotland)	12 Aug. 1871	Maharajah Duleep Singh	440 Grouse (Over Dogs)
Hunt Hill (Scotland)	14 Aug. 1887	Captain Tomasson	458 Grouse (Over Dogs)

	Rhinoceros	Tiger	Buffalo	Sambur	Pig	Deer	Red Deer	Grouse	Partridges	Pheasants	Woodcock	Snipe	Wild Duck	Black Game	Capercailzie	Hares	Rabbits	Various	Total
1867							8	265	1179	741	20	22	10			719	934	115	4013
1868							35	201	1418	1601	28	67	23			690	543	113	4719
1869							35	135	1659	1431	26	133	37			547	443	122	4568
1870							21	498	2309	2117	36	53	30			833	626	137	6660
1871							55	1408	1598	1859	80	244	42			1093	341	225	6945
1872							38	1498	2083	2835	27	60	31			1108	756	235	8671
1873							25	248	2417	3050	95	263	85			1027	450	591	8251
1874				3			5	90	2878	2345	229	462	131	5	4	1200	302	1200	8854
1875							3	287	2882	3225	176	461	208			1376	576	743	9937
1876							3	1551	3394	4110	30	25	37			1245	890	266	11,551
1877					2		4	2032	2359	4235	35	45	33	11	11	1496	1044	309	11,616
1878					4		9	1669	3378	4679	43	44	55	5	6	2157	662	503	13,214
1879							4	1344	630	3140	132	92	62	9	11	1125	287	215	7051
1880		9	6	18	31	73	12	1131	682	531	9	47	54	26	5	501	141	408	3684
1881							5	1566	3465	5014	26	14	43			1058	791	166	12,148
1882	2	2	6	1	66	104	10	3025	2123	2370	14	21	44			464	1122	117	9491
1883							5	2896	1845	6119	157	84	155			918	1386	319	13,884
1884							10	3073	3523	4347	134	70	70			713	1896	453	14,289
1885							5	2015	2788	4620	104	23	31			589	2547	108	12,830
1886							20	1989	1463	3383	105	87	72			357	786	349	8611
1887							57	2258	3785	3387	104	3	12			415	2328	237	12,586
1888							4	3060	853	5072	31	151	10			307	1523	85	11,096
1889							5	3081	5751	6182	100	109	14	38	8	1747	1069	135	18,239
1890								2006	7002	6498	172	105	28			1446	1120	123	18,500
1891								2277	1699	5794	34	13				711	406	271	11,205
1892							1	1412	6784	5580	7	10	5			453	1233	281	15,766
1893								2611	8732	5760	66	7	42			837	914	166	19,135
1894							1	2567	7261	5034	76	7	12			935	580	222	16,695
1895							1	1272	3461	6101	11	13	17			352	1040	210	12,478
1896								2649	2613	8514	13	11	4			314	557	177	14,852
1897							1	2797	1914	7850	67	10	47			358	828	152	14,024
1898								1693	1200	3432	18	3	6			169	298	144	6963
1899								823	1309	4605	16	2	57			205	609	137	7763
1900								1033	1322	6762	24	8	95			223	819	141	10,427
1901								2037	1991	8478	8	11	141			262	595	114	13,637
1902								1706	1701	4998	11	3	166			268	479	280	9612
1903								1890	462	4709	16	3	213			206	647	111	8257
1904								1355	1794	5032	17	13	127			186	173	114	8811
1905								1636	2292	6939	15	11	111			258	582	206	12,050
1906								2179	2019	8647	22	12	268			230	416	212	14,005
1907								1268	477	4386	15	7	111			88	152	144	6648
1908								1523	364	5764	29	9	129			159	183	176	8316
1909								2036	653	6374	25	15	115			155	195	195	9763
1910								1923	770	6115	24	12	155			150	89	234	9472
1911								2036	978	6463	23	5	59			158	143	191	10,056
1912								1810	518	7539	18	1	103			251	409	45	10,694
1913								1461	820	5179	13	11	172			243	223	121	8233
1914								2385	1628	4434									
1915								3078	2596	2598									
1916								3435	613	895									
1917								2087	1159	1990									
1918								1445	878	1279									
1919								1097	1151	1185									
1920								765	685	1527									
1921								1984	1342	2081									
1922								982	1387	2289									
1923								915	356										
									124,193	241,224									556,813

Appendix 2
Lord Ripon on How to Shoot

To be a first-rate shot necessitates the combination of two distinctly opposite conditions: a highly strung nervous temperament which keeps you ever on the alert, a cool head which enable you in moments of excitement to fire without recklessness or undue haste. This combination is naturally rare. That 'practice makes perfect' is in the case of shooting' only true to a certain extent, for a man must be born with a certain inherent aptitude to become a really first-rate shot.

The great thing for a beginner is not to lose heart, and to those who realise that proficiency in any art means hard work and perseverance, I offer the following suggestions, which are the result of long experience.

One of the first points to be considered is that of standing so as to be prepared for every variety of shot. If the bird is flying to your right, your left leg should be forward: if to the left, your right leg. This is most important, and I have improved the shooting of several of my friends quite twenty-five per cent by showing them how to stand.

Quickness in letting off the second or even the third gun is no doubt to a great extent a matter of practice. Never look at your gun or your loader, for while your hands should be ever ready to receive the gun from him, your eyes should be concentrated on the birds. A quick shooter will fire his two guns and four barrels almost as if they were on one stock.

It is also most necessary to acquire and cultivate judgment of distance. Some men never know if a bird is forty or sixty yards off, others are apt to consider the object out of shot when it is not more than fifty yards from the muzzle of the gun.

When birds are coming in great numbers, always select one to shoot at, and do not vacillate, whatever happens. Many men who are good shots at single birds miss when they are obliged to choose one out of a lot to fire at, simply from inability to make up their minds in time It is a question of quick selection and judgment, the latter quality being also all-important in the case of the *angle* at which the bird should be shot. Nearly ever shooter has his favourite angle – that is to say, given plenty of time, he shoots at his bird when it reaches the angle he prefers; but this tendency can be carried too far and should not be encouraged, for a man often gets into the habit of waiting for those birds which present themselves according to his fancy, and neglecting the shots he finds difficult, which are obviously those which he should practise most.

One of the most puzzling shots is the dropping bird which does not move its wings, for unconsciously the movement of the wings assists the shooter in judging the pace at which the bird is flying, and when it is soaring the pace is very difficult to estimate. Lord Walsingham holds that the best way of hitting a bird of this kind is to snap at it as one would at a rabbit, and I am of his opinion. It is easier to judge the speed of a bird's flight after it has passed; but the shooter should always fire at it first as it approaches him, otherwise he loses time, and will never head the list at a big shoot.

When a bird flies high and steadily, the easiest angle is the perpendicular one, that is to say, straight over the shooter's head; but here again, if he waits for this angle he loses the chance of getting a second shot with turning round.

Aiming at the bird's head, and tipping the gun forward at the moment of firing, is sometimes advocated, but I, personally, do not approve of this method. When the bird has passed, the aim must be taken below, and very much below, where it is flying high. This is by no means easy, and the natural tendency is to shoot over, that is to say, behind the bird.

The curling bird, which flies in a half circle, should be aimed at very quickly on the inside curve of its flight, and the gun fired as it reaches the shoulder.

The cross shot, the most useful of all for driving purposes, should be taken well in front, rather above the bird, with a strong swing.

Now *Swing* is one of the secrets of good shooting. The gun should be moved as far as can be judged at the same pace as that at which the bird or beast is travelling. The swing should continue after the charge has left the barrel, just as a golf club or a billiard cue should continue to follow the course which the ball takes after it has been struck. Both eyes should be kept open, the left hand well forward along the barrel, but not so forward as to risk straining the muscles of the back or arms, always taking care not to drop the muzzle at the moment of pulling the trigger; the legs in the position described on the previous page.

When you are placed in a butt or behind a wall, it is very necessary that either should be so arranged as to hide you as much as possible, whilst allowing you plenty of freedom of action.

In the case of a circular butt, it is wise to pull down a good deal of the back part so as to facilitate your shooting at birds which have passed flying low.

In partridge driving, when standing up to a hedge or wall, it is all important that these should be of the right height. They generally require heightening or lowering. Twigs or boughs should be bound down or raised in the hedges, and stones should be removed from, or replaced on, the walls, so as to ensure a comfortable screen for shooting.

I also lay great stress on the importance of keeping quiet during a drive, as birds are wonderfully quick at detecting any movement or sound. People often say to me, 'The birds seem to avoid me and fly over you.' The reason is that I have kept quiet till the moment of firing, while my neighbours have been laughing, talking, jumping about, and really acting as flankers to me. This advice may appear to be of a most elementary nature, but it is remarkable how often the simple precaution it advocates is disregarded.

I will conclude these few remarks on the *technique* of shooting, which I proffer for what they are worth, with my favourite maxim: '*Aim high, keep the gun moving, and never check,*' for it is one which has proved immensely serviceable to me all through my life. I cannot, however, dismiss the subject of shooting altogether without alluding to that side of it which appeals so strongly to every true sportsman, and that is the close contact into which it brings him with nature. To be really interested in shooting means a knowledge and study of woodcraft, of the habits and ways of bird and beast. The legislation which is levelled against the owners of land is doing its best to destroy the old type of country gentleman in whom the love of sport and nature has always been indissolubly united. To him the crow of the grouse as he speeds along the purple heather, or the guttural note of the pheasant as he flies across the crimson sky on a winter's afternoon brings with them a sense of joyous exultation; and the moors, fields, hedgerows, and woods sheltering myriads of winged and four-footed creatures, are for him full of potential and indefinable charm.

Maybe a generation will spring up to whom all these things will be a closed book; but when that day comes England will lose her most attractive and distinctive feature, and one of her most cherished traditions. For the England of whom the poets have sung for many centuries will have ceased to exist.'

Reprinted from *King Edward VII as a Sportsman*, by Alfred E. T. Watson, Longman, Green & Co., 1911.

Index

Numbers in italic indicate an illustration.

Aberdeen, Lady
    Memories of a Scottish Grannie, 60
Adolphus of Teck, Prince, 58
Advertisement for 1910, *13*
Ailesbury, Lady, 87, 127
Albania, 70
Albemarle, Lady, 67
Albemarle, Lord, 66, 69, *84-85,* 107
Albert, Prince (later King George VI) 16
Alexandra, Princess (later Queen), *19,*
    25, 29, 36, 57, 82, 84
Alfonso, King XIII, of Spain, 70, *80,* 81
Alington, Lord, 97
Anson, Sir John, 16
Ashburton, Lord, 50, 69, *91*
Asquith, Herbert, first Earl of Oxford
    and Asquith, 66-67
Astor, Lady Violet, *100*
Austria, 79
Austria, The Emperor of, 60

Bacchante, HMS, 27
Bachelor's Cottage, Sandringham, 27
Bacon, Roger, 13
Baden-Baden, 73
Badminton Library, 8-9
Badminton Series, The (Gallwey and
    Walsingham), 41
Bagot, Mr., 77
Bailey's Magazine,
    list of 12 best game shots in Britain,
    50
Balfour, Arthur (later Lord Balfour),
    48, 65, *65*
Balfour, Edith, 46
Balmoral, 20, 29, 78, 104, 115-116
Bankes, Ralph, 96
Baring, Lady Evelyn, 67
Battue, 70, 116
Beaters, *see* Shooting
Beatrice, Princess, 99
Bedford, The Duchess of, 88

Beresford, Lord Charles, 100
Blenheim Palace, *64-65,* 64-66, 92, 97
Bluberhouse Moor, 50
Bohemia, 75
Bolsover, Lady, 113
Bradgate, 130
British Museum, The, 48
Brooke, Lady, 19, 82
Brunsdon, Mr (Sandringham), 120
Burnham, Lord, 23-24, *24,* 67, 83
Bustard, Great, 78

Cadogan, Lady, 84
Cahir, Scotland, 127
Calder, Sir James, 25
Canisy, Count, *106*
Cardigan, Lady, 78
Cardigan, Lord, 78
Carlos, King of Portugal, 79
Carnarvon, Lord, 50, 131
Cartridge boys, *120,* 121
Casa de Campo, 70
Cassano Orchestra, The, 96
Cassel, Sir Ernest, 84, 131
Castle Antrim, 128
Castle Museum, Norwich, 48
Castle Rising, 20
Cawdor Moors, 126
Chamberlain, Joseph, 60
Chaplin, Harry, 21-22, 44, *44,* 51, 64-65
Chatsworth, 36, 60, *61, 63,* 65-66, 82, 90,
    99
Chester, The Bishop of, 100
Churchill, Lord Randolph, 65
Clarence, The Duke of, 16, 23, 27
Clark, Sir James, *38*
Clarke, Nellie, 19
Clay pigeon trophy, Isle of Wight, 81
Cleveland, The Duchess of, 110
Cleveland, The Duke of, 47, 108, 110
 Coke of Norfolk', 57
Coke, Mr, (The Squire of Holkham),
    112
Cole, Lord, 113
Colman, Russell, *69*
Combe Abbey, 74, *121*

Commodore Woods, 35
Connaught, The Duke of, 104, 116, 128
Consort, The Prince, 19, 36-37, 85
Cornwallis-West, George, 47, 96, 119
Cotterell, Sir John, *98*
Country Life, advertisement, *102*
Coventry, 60
Coventry, Lord and Lady, 99, 100
Coventry, The Hon. Mrs. Henry, *93*
Cowper, The Hon. Spencer, 26
Craven, Lord, 74, 123
Creswell Crags, 64
Crichel, 20, 97, *120*
Croquet, A Game of, *21*
Curzon, George, 65
Curzon, Lady, *89*
Cusker, Hughie, 92
Cust, Sir Charles, 35, 88, 100
Cust, Harry, 82
Czar of Russia, The, *106*

Darwin, Charles, 8
de Grey, *see* Lord Ripon
de Grey, Tom, *see* Walsingham, the 6th
    Lord
de Poucins, The Vicomte Lailly
    Loriet, 92, 94
de Soveral, The Marquis, 62, *82-83,*
    82
Derby, Lord, *36*
Dersingham Woods, 35
Desborough, Lord, 69
Devonshire, The Duchess of, (formerly
    Duchess of Manchester), 61
Devonshire, The 8th Duke of,
    courtesy title of Marquess of Harting-
    ton and nicknamed 'Harty Tarty',
    60-62
Devonshire House Ball, The, 61
Dorchester, Lord, 50
D'Orleans, The Duc, 26
D'Orsay, The Countess, 26
Duck, *see* Shooting
Dudley, Lord, *107,* 122

Edenhall, 112
Edward VII, King, (formerly the Prince of Wales), *19, 21*
  and Abbot of Tepl, 75
  and Duke of Connaught, 116
  and guests, 78
  and head keeper at Sandringham, *31*
  and Lord Leicester, 57
  and Order of the Garter, 61-62
  and red grouse, 28
  and shooting, 71
  and *Tailor and Cutter*, 103
  as gourmet, 83-85
  as house guest, 95-96
  as sportsman, *20*
  as Squire of Sandringham, *32*
  at Elveden, 23
  at Merton, 48
  at Quidenham, 69
  at Sandringham, *23*, 26-27, 31-32, *33*, 35
  at Six Mile Bottom, 131
  at Tulchan, 50
  at West Dean, 96-97
  at Windsor, 37, *38*, 106
  birthday shoot, 29-30, 35
  croquet game, 21-22
  favourite loader, 124
  firing Maxim Gun at Wimbledon, 22
  first shots, 16
  in Scotland, *20*
  influence on shooting, 60
  introduction of Virginia Quail to Norfolk, 27
  leader of Society, 19
  life in Norfolk, 25
  love of shooting, 11, 19, 20-21
  near East tour, 20
  nicknamed 'tum-tum', 31
  no temperament for hunting, 11
  picnic lunches, 87
  practical joker, 60
  provision of social impetus, 18
  purchase of Sandringham, 17, 25
  regulations for those shooting at Sandringham, 107
  search for estate, 25
  Set, 47, 57
  shooting skill, 20-21
  shooting in Germany, 73
  shooting in other countries, 70
  shooting with Lord Stamford, 130
  strain of office, 82
  views on dress, 103, 105
  visiting tomb of Rameses IV, 70
  visit to Blenheim, 65
  visits to Marienbad, 73
  wedding, 19
  Wolferton Station built for guests, 17
Edward VIII, (formerly the Prince of Wales, 53
King Edward VII as a Sportsman (A. E. T. Watson), 137-139
Edwardian Society, 105-106
Egypt, 70

Eichhorn, 71
Elveden, 20, 23, 36, 55, 60, 79, 88, 100, 105, 116
Elveden System, The, 11
Essex Hunt Races, The, 19
Estates, *see* under individual names
Euston Station, London, 16, *18*
Euston System, The, 11

Fane, Lady Augusta, 96
Fasque, Kincardineshire, 119
Fellowes, Sir Ailwyn, 93
Ferdinand, The Archduke Franz, 72-73, 79
Field, The, 28, 94
Fife, The Duke of, 116
Fingall, Lady, 31, 73, 84, 88, 100
Fishbourne, Polly (Keeper), 111-112
Fleetwood, 18
Flemish Farm, 36
Flitcham Farm, 35
Fountains Abbey, 69
Four Generations, see Quiller Orchardson
Francis of Teck, Prince, 82
Frewen, Moreton, 129-130
Fursenstein, 90

Gallwey, Sir Ralph Payne, 8, 41-43, *41, 44*, 94, 96
  see also, *Badminton Series*
  High Pheasants in Theory and Practice
  Letters to Young Shooters
Gamekeepers, *110*, 111, *111*, 112, *112*, 113, 115-116, *117, 118*, 118-120
Gamekeeper (lady), 111, *111*, 112
Garnier, Mrs William, 88
George I, 36
George V, King (formerly the Prince of Wales and Duke of York), *15*, 15-16, 23-24, 27, 37, 40, 50, 58-59, 88, 104, *104*, 125
Germany, 73
Gladstone, H. S., 92
Gladstone Estate, 119
Golden Valley Drive at Warter, The, 67
Gosfords, The, 65
Grandtully Estate, The, Perthshire, 55
Grant, Arthur, 116
Grant, John, 116
Grenfell, Julian, 69
Grenfells, The, 65
Grey, Charles, *38*
Grey, Major, *38*
Grouse shooting, *113*
Guinness, Sir Edward, *see* Lord Iveagh
Gun,
  breech loader, 15
  development of, 13, 15
  duelling, 15
  hammer, *14*, 15
  percussion, 15
  shotgun, 15
Gurney, Sir Somerville, 107

Haakon, King of Norway, *39*
Hall Barn, 20-21, 67, 83
Hares, *see* Shooting
Hartington, Lord, 60-61, 64
Hartington, The Marquess of, *see* the 8th Duke of Devonshire
'Harty Tarty' at Devonshire House Ball, *62*
Hawking as a sport, 13
Henniker, Lord, 69
Hibbert, Mr Washington, 18
Highclere, *131*
High Force Moor, 47
High Pheasants in Theory and Practice (Gallwey), 41
Himley, 129
Hirsch, The Baron, 35, *71*, 71, 73, 75
Hirsch estate, The, 70
Holford, Sir George, 131
Holkham, 20, 27, 30, 36, 56-58, 60, 86, *86*, 111, 118
Holkham, The Squire of (Mr Coke), 112
Holkham Hall, *56*
Holland, Lady, 26
Houghton, Lord, 106
Howe, George, 47
Howe, Lord, 67
Hungary, 75
Huntingfield, Lord, 69

India, 70
Ireland, 91-92, 128
Isle of Wight, 78, 81
Isle of Wight, Clay Pigeon Trophy, 81
Iveagh, Lord (formerly Sir Edward Guinness), 56, 91-92

Jackson, Mr, *31*, 35, 120
Jakse, Carl, 122-123
James, Edward, *107*
James, Mrs Willie, *107*
James, Willie, 107
Jameson, Mrs Willie, 73, 90

Kaiser, The, *37*, 73, 81
Karolyi, Count Louis, 73
Keith Hall, *94-95*, 109
Keppel, Mrs Alice, *32*, 69
Keppel, Sir Derek, 116
Keppel, Sir Harry, 36
Kintore, Lord, 95
Kintore, Lord (Visitors Book), *109*
Kingston Lacy, 96
Kirkcaldy, Andrew, 122
Knowsley, 88
Knutsford, Lord, 32
Koh-i-noor diamond, The, 55
Kour, Maharanee Jinda, The, 55

Lancastre, The Count of, 78
Langwell, 112
Latimer, Bishop, 11
Laycock, Joe, 82
Leadenhall Market, 133
Legge, Harry, 35

Leicester, The Earl and Countess of, 30
Leicester, Lord (the first), 58
Leicester, Lord, 27, 31, 57, 57, 58, 58, 59, 59, 86, 94
Leslie, Sir Shane, 108
Letellier, Madame, 22
Letters to Young Shooters (Gallwey), 41
Leveson-Gower, Lady Florence, 16
Lichnowsky, Herr, 66-67
Literary Society, The, 48
Liverpool Evening News, The, 87
Loaders' duties, 121-126
Londonderry, Lord, 66-67
Londonderrys, The, 65-66
Londoners, weekending by train, 17
Lonsdale, Lord, 81
Lonsdale, Lady (later de Grey), 44-45
Loreburn, Lord, 106
Louise, Princess, 99
Lowther, 81
Lynford estate, 25

Mac-Calmont, Lady, *90*
MaClean, James, 117
Mahaffy, Professor, 108
Manchester, The Duchess of, *see* under Duchess of Devonshire
Manoel, 11, King of Portugal, 79
Marienbad, 21, 73-75, 103
Marlborough, The Duchess of, 36, 45, 92, 97
Marlborough, The Duke of, 64-65, 92
Marvell, Andrew, 43
Massereene and Ferrard, Lord, 128-129
Meklenburg-Strelitz, The Grand Duchess of, 60
Mellanistic Mutant pheasant, 116
Memories of a Scottish Grannie, see Lady Aberdeen
Merton Hall, 8, 20, 47-48, 50, 85
Milbank, Sir Frederick, 88, 90
Montagu, George, 13, 15
Monte Carlo, 45, 90
Montenegro, 77
Motor cars, *128-129*
Motteux, John, 26
Motteux, Peter Anthony, 26
Mount Juliet, 90
Musgrave, Sir George, 112

Natural History Museum, The, 48
Newlands, 101
Niagara Falls, 69
Norfolk, Wild Turkey shooting, 27
North Runcton Hall, 107
Norwich, Castle Museum, 48
Nunburnholme, Lord, 67

Old Beckenham Hall, 108
Orchardson, Quiller, (*Four Generations*), 103
Osborne House, Isle of Wight, 19
Overton, Mr, 39-40
Oxford, Earl of, *see* Horace Walpole
Oyster Banquets, London, 83

Panshanger, 46, 49
Pelham-Clinton, Lord Edward, 38
Pembroke, Lord, 78
Pepys, Samuel, *Diary*, 14
Perthshire, shooting, 18
Pheasants, 116-118
    see also Mellanstic Mutant pheasant
Pirrie, Lord, 117
Pless, Princess Daisy of, 82, 90, 99, 101
Poklewski-Koziell, Monsieur, 78
Ponsonby, Captain, Fritz, 21-22, 37-38, 73, 74, 74-75, 78, 99, 110
Portland, The 5th Duke of, 16, 35-36, 40, 60, 72, 106, 112-113, 115, 122, 133
Portugal, The King of, 62
Powder,
    smokeless introduced, 15
Prince, Mr, 125
Prince of Wales, *see* King Edward VII
Probyn, General Sir Dighton, V.C., 34
Puccini, Giacomo,
    duck shooting, 76
Purdey, Athol,
    gunmaker, 15

Quail, Virginia, 27-28
Quidenham, 20, 69, 85, *117*

Rabbit shoot, 92
Raby, 108
Radziwill, Princess, 88
Railway development, 16
Railway, opening of Glasgow and Gainkirk, 1831, *16*
Railway station, typical country, 1900, *17*
Raine, Edward, 112
Record shoot, 1913, 24
Remise system, 35
Rendlesham, Lord, 28
Retrievers, 72-73
Ripon, the 1st Marquess of, Viceroy of India, 43
Ripon, the 2nd Marquess of (formerly Lord de Grey), 7, *44*, 45, *46-47*, 47, 59
    and loader, 126
    at Blenheim, 66
    at Bradgate, 130
    at St Johann, 73
    at Sandringham, 46, 51
    at Studley Royal, 69
    at Warter, 67
    at Windsor, 106
    bag, 15
    dinner parties, 45
    game killed, 1867-1923, 135
    greatest shot in England, 43-44
    how to shoot, 137-139
    in *Bailey's Magazine* list, 50
    marriage to Gladys Lonsdale, 44
    preparation for shooting, 92
    shooting anecdotes, 50
    shooting skill, 50
    speed of shooting, 52

use of hammer guns, 15
use of smokeless powder, 15
wearing spats, 104
writing on shooting, 52
Ritz Hotel site sold, 48
Robinson, Peter, 124-125
Robinson, Miss Queenie, *108*
Robinson, Mr (loader), 33
Rosebery, Lord, 51, 63, 110
Ross, Donald, 112-113, 115
Rossmore, Lord, 23, 91-92, 101, 104-105, 128
Rothschild, Lord, 116
Rufford Abbey, 67, *88*
Russell, Lady Frankland, 48
Rutland, The Duke of, *103*

St Johann, 71
St Pancras Station, London, 31
Sandringham, 20, 25-26, 29, 31, 125
    and ladies, 87
    and Lady Ailesbury, 127
    and Lord Ripon, 46
    and Lord Suffield, 105
    beaters, 120
    Bohemian Band, The, 71
    bowling alley, 34
    competitive spirit, 51
    dispute, 26
    drawing room, *30*
    game book, 16
    game card, *34*
    houseparty, 28-29, 36
    keeper of the kennels (Mr Brunsdon), 120
    lunches, 86-87
    pheasants and partridges, 29, 48
    pheasant rearing, 11
    pheasantries, *13*
    purchase of estate, 17, 25
    King Edward VII's regulations for shooting, 107
    remise system of rearing partridges, 71
    rules for house parties, 31
    science of keepers, 120
    shoots, 11
    standard of shooting, 35, 56
    tea parties, 36
    wild game, 11
    York Cottage, 27
Sarajevo, 79
Sassoons, The, 50
Savile, Lord, 67, 88
Scarborough Clump, 58, *58*, 86
Scarborough Wood, 58-59
Scott, Sir Walter, 118
Schultz, Colonel, 15
Schwalbach, 73
Seymour, General, *38*
She Stoops to Conquer, 99
Shooting,
    art of, 13-14
    beaters, 120-121, *122-125*, 127-129, 131

distinctive dress of, 129
in Ireland, 128-129
strike at Cahir, Scotland, 127
brake, *101*
driven, development of, 54
duck, 75, *76*, 77
hares, 72-73
hazards, 14
houseparties, 94-96, 101, 103
in England, (between 1870 and 1914),
    52
in Scotland, 18
loaders, 121-126
lunches, 83
organised, 13
parties, *10, 12*, 103-105
people on estates involved, 126-127
problems, 77-78
tea parties, 91
techniques, 71-73
weeks, 82
Singer, Mr, 126
Singh, The Maharajah, Duleep, 11, 28,
    50, *53*, 54-56
Singh, Prince Freddy, 56
Singh, Prince Victor Duleep, *54*, *56*, 56
Singh, Ranjit, 54-55
Singhs, The Duleep, 66, 92, 104, 116
Six Mile Bottom, 131
Spaniels, Clumber, 39
Spanish Ambassador, The, 37
Sportsman's Directory, The, 13
Stamford, Lord, 130
Stonor, Eddy, 75
Stonor, Sir Harry, 35, 50, *51-52*, 66-67
Stonor Park, *114-115*
Studley Royal, *45*, 45, 50, 69, 109
Studley Royal, game cart, *127*
Sweden, 78
Swedish peasant, 77
Suffield, Lord, 105
Sutherland, The Duke of, 16-17, 80-81
Syracuse, 75

Tables of Game shot at individual
    shoots, 134
Tailor and Cutter, 103
Tariol-Baugé, Anna, *70*
Tennyson, Lord, 78
Tepl, The Abbot of, 74
Thetford, 28
Thirkleby gun room, *43*
Thirkleby Hall, Thirsk, 41-43
Thirkleby shooting card, *42*
Torre del Lago, 76
Totmagyar, 73
Trautmansdorff, The Count, 70
Tring, 116-117
Tulchan, 50
Turner, Tommy, 56

Vane-Tempest, Lord Bertie, 17, 67, *68*
Vernon, Miss Di, 108
Victoria, Queen, 19, 44, 55, 57, 85, 88,
    99
Victoria, Princess, 88
Visitors' Book, 108, *109*, 110
Vizianagram, The Dewan of, 70

Waldegrave, Lady, 60
Wallace, Alfred Russell, 8
Walpole, Horace (later the Earl of
    Oxford), 60
Walsingham, The 5th Lord, 111
Walsingham, The 6th Lord, 7, 43, 47,
    49, 50
Walsingham, Lord,
  accident with powder, 15
  and British Museum, 48
  and Castle Museum, Norwich, 48
  and red grouse, 28
  and Sandringham, 27
  bankruptcy caused by shooting, 11
  best way of hitting bird, 138
  character, 48
  finances, 48, 55
  greatest shot in England, 41, 47
  record bag, 50
  shooting skill, 50

shooting record, 7-8, 50
speed of shooting, 52
stamina, 92
use of hammer guns, 15
see also Badminton series
Walsingham House, 8
Walters, Miss Catherine, 60
Watson, A. E. T. (*King Edward* VII *as
    a Sportsman*), 137-139
Watts, Mr, 70
Warter Priory, 67, *89*, 112, *124-125*
Warwick, Daisy, 91
Warwick, Lord, 8, 20-21, 23, 85, 88, 95,
    126, 133
Welbeck Estate, 20, 72, 79, 129
Wemyss, Lord, 47
West Dean, 20, 96, *107*, 107
Westley Richards Hammer Gun, The,
    14
Westmorland, The Dowager Lady, 87
Whitley Park, 117
Wildfowling, *119*
Willan, Mr, 29, *104*, 116
William the Conqueror, 36
William III, 123
Williams, Mrs. Hwfa, 67, 90-91
Willoughby de Broke, Lord, 67
Willoughby, Sir John, 47
Wilson, R. H. Rimington, 50
Wilton House, Wiltshire, 78, *104*
Windsor (formerly Wyndleshora), 14,
    19, 25, 29, 36-38, *38*, 39, *40*, 70, 75,
    79, 81, 85, 87, 95, 106
Winterhalter painting at Windsor, 38
Wolferton Heath, 28
Wolferton railway station, 17, 31, 87
Wombell, Stephen, 92
Wyndleshora, *see* Windsor
Wynyard, 65-66

York Cottage, Sandringham, 27
York, The Duke of, *see* King George V
Yorkshire Heathland, 28